CHILDREN OF THE LIVING GOD

By the same author:
The Christian Life
Deserted by God?
Grow in Grace
Healthy Christian Growth
A Heart for God
John Owen on the Christian Life
Let's Study Mark
Let's Study Philippians
The Pundit's Folly
Read Any Good Books?
The Sermon on the Mount

CHILDREN OF THE LIVING GOD

SINCLAIR B. FERGUSON

THE BANNER OF TRUTH TRUST

THE BANNER OF TRUTH TRUST
3 Murrayfield Road, Edinburgh, EH12 6EL
PO Box 621, Carlisle, Pennsylvania 17013, USA

★

©*Sinclair B. Ferguson 1989*
First published 1989
Reprinted 2005
ISBN 0 85151 536 3

★

Set in 10 1/2/12pt Linotron Plantin
Typeset at The Spartan Press Ltd,
Lymington, Hants
and printed and bound in the USA by
Versa Press, Inc.,
East Peoria, IL

★

Contents

FOR
DAVID AND PETER
JOHN AND RUTH

If the love of a father will not make a child delight in him, what will?

John Owen (1616–1683)

Preface

You cannot open the pages of the New Testament without realising that one of the things that makes it so 'new', in every way, is that here men and women call God 'Father'. This conviction, that we can speak to the Maker of the universe in such intimate terms, lies at the heart of the Christian faith. Through Christ, says Paul, we have 'access to the Father' (*Eph. 2:18*). References to God as Father are exceedingly rare in the Old Testament. By contrast there are over two hundred *different* references to God as Father scattered throughout the New Testament. That is an astonishing testimony to the new sense of God's grace that came with the message of the gospel.

Yet the Christian church in general has not always maintained this fresh and living sense of the Fatherhood of God. It has often failed to appreciate that the Christian life is a life of sonship.

Prior to the great evangelical awakening of the sixteenth century (better known to us as the Reformation), the popular view of the Christian life was one of fear and bondage rather than of sonship. Luther, of course, broke through this decay of Christianity with his discovery of justification by faith alone. But for Luther (and for many others since) the idea that we are also made sons and daughters of God was often hidden by the bright glow of our justification by faith. Indeed, only occasionally has sonship been seen as much more than a subsidiary, if positive, element in the Christian life. Many of the standard evangelical textbooks of theology (which inform and shape the minds of those who teach the gospel to the church and the world) give only a few lines to the subject of sonship. It is, therefore, little wonder if we do not enter into our privileges as fully as we might.

Not only has the subject of sonship been neglected, but in the past century 'liberal' theology has placed such an emphasis on the *universal Fatherhood of God*, and the *universal brotherhood of man*, that evangelical Christians have (understandably, if mistakenly) tended to keep well clear of teaching, preaching, or writing on this theme. There have been some notable exceptions, including the American Southern Presbyterian theologians J. L. Girardeau and R. A. Webb, the Southern Baptist R. L. Dagg, and the distinguished Scottish theologian R. S. Candlish. But they wrote in long-distant days. There is certainly a need for their work to be developed and further elucidated.

It is not my purpose in this book to write in the erudite style of these authors. I have a humbler vision, but one that is no less important: to begin to recommunicate to the living church the privileges and responsibilities of being able to call God 'Father'. My purpose is, however, not too far removed from that of my fellow countryman R. S. Candlish, who wrote of his lectures, published under the title *The Fatherhood of God*:

My object is chiefly a practical one. It is to bring out the import and bearing of the Scriptural doctrine respecting the Fatherhood of God, as an influential element in Christian experience.[1]

Children of the Living God looks at this same Christian experience, but from the standpoint of our sonship as well as God's Fatherhood. Of all biblical pictures of what it means to be a Christian, this one is as crucial for our times as it is central to the Christian gospel. My hope is that in some way, these pages will cause more and more reflection on the great privileges that are ours in Christ Jesus.

SINCLAIR B. FERGUSON
Westminster Theological Seminary
Philadelphia, Pennsylvania

[1] R. S. Candlish, *The Fatherhood of God* (Edinburgh: A. and C. Black, 1866), p. 5.

1
The Children
of God

I was going through a series of interviews for a new appointment. One was to focus on my spiritual life. I vividly remember one of the interviewers asking me, 'How would you describe your relationship with God?'

I was not very clear about what he meant. Was he asking whether I had spent time in Bible reading and prayer earlier in the day? Or was he wanting to know if I was harbouring some secret sin, clouding my sense of fellowship with God? He explained that he really meant: 'What terms would you use to describe yourself in relation to God?' After a moment's thought I replied, 'As a servant. And, yes, as a son!'

The series of interviews was tiring, and at the end of the day someone else was offered the job. But in a sense that did not matter very much, because I had found myself saying something that echoed and re-echoed in my mind for days afterwards. Perhaps it was simply the fact that I had never been asked that question before. Perhaps it was because I had never articulated the answer in quite the same way. But, whatever the reason, it had dawned on me with an altogether new sense of wonder: I was nothing less than a child of the living God! He was a Father to me. I knew that I was a son to him. What a privilege!

This is exactly what the apostle John wanted his fellow Christians to sense when he wrote:

> How great is the love the Father has lavished on us, that we should be called children of God! And that is what we are! . . . Dear friends, now we are children of God, and what we will be has not yet been made known. But we know that when he appears, we shall be like him, for we shall see him as he is (*1 Jn. 3:1-2*).

The conviction behind this book is that realising what John was speaking about is life-transforming. It lies at the heart of understanding the whole of the Christian life and all of the diverse elements in our daily experience. It is *the* way – not the *only* way, but the *fundamental* way – for the Christian to think about himself or herself. Our self-image, if it is to be biblical, will begin just here. God is my Father (the Christian's self-image always begins with the knowledge of *God* and *who he is*!); I am one of his children (I know my real identity); his people are my brothers and sisters (I recognise the family to which I belong, and have discovered my deepest 'roots').

Do you think about yourself and the Christian life in this way? It is more common for Christians to think of their experience in terms of what our forefathers called the 'order of salvation' – a series of distinct, but connected, events or experiences. Usually that order of experience would begin with regeneration, faith, and repentance, and go on to sanctification, perseverance, and glorification. The 'order of salvation' was an attempt to trace the different stages of the work of the Holy Spirit in our lives.

Sometimes focusing our attention in this way on our own experiences in the process of salvation can misfire, especially if by natural disposition we are introspective and doubting. We may begin to ask, 'What stage have I reached? Did I really experience the earlier stages properly? Was I deeply enough convicted of sin (like John Bunyan, or Martin Luther, or Augustine, about whom we may have been reading)?' Of course, self-examination does have a proper place in the Christian life. But morbid introspection, or doubting, is a very different thing, especially since we already know that 'nothing good lives in me, that is, in my sinful nature' (*Rom. 7:18*).

Our thinking about *who we are as Christians* should not begin with what we can discover about ourselves by self-analysis. Rather, it begins with what God says about those who trust in Christ.

One of the most interesting things about the teaching of the New Testament is that, in several key passages that summarise the purposes of God throughout history and in our individual lives, salvation is described as membership in the family of God. We are God's sons and daughters, his free-born children. Being a Christian is not dependent on experiences so much as on our new relationship with God.

A NEW TESTAMENT EMPHASIS

Several central passages in the New Testament stress our sonship with God the Father. For example, Galatians 3:26–4:7 (probably Paul's earliest letter) describes Christian experience against the background of God's purposes in history. Paul contrasts spiritual experience before and after Christ's coming. Is there any difference? There certainly is! It is like the difference between being a child, with all the restrictions and rules of childhood, and becoming a grown-up son, with all the freedoms, privileges and resources that implies.

Paul says there is an underlying unity in God's way of salvation in Old and New Testament times (as Paul's illustration of Abraham, in Romans 4:1–12 and Galatians 3:6–9, proves). But there is also a dramatic development realised in the coming of Christ. In terms of experience it is like the difference between being restricted by guardians and trustees (remember the dark figure of the 'guardian' in the children's stories you used to read?), and inheriting the family fortune! When Paul paints the picture of salvation with a broad brush, he finds the picture of the Christian as a grown-up son at the heart of it.

Further on, in Ephesians 1:3–6 (probably Paul's most general letter), Christian experience is traced from its origin in the eternal purpose of God to its goal in the praise of the glory and grace of God – 'He chose us in him [Christ] before the creation of the world to be holy and blameless in his sight . . . to the praise of his glorious grace.' But what is God's purpose in all this? 'In love he predestined us to be adopted as his sons through Jesus Christ.' The creation of a family, with children, is the reason for all of God's activity. This is how he intends to show his glory.

Two further passages underline that the purpose of the incarnation of God's Son is the creation of the family of God. He took our flesh and entered a world of sin, suffering, and rebellion against God, in order that he might be 'made like his brothers in every way' (*Heb. 2:17*). Why should this be? Again Paul provides the answer: 'For those God foreknew he also predestined to be conformed to the likeness of his Son, *that he might be the firstborn among many brothers*' (*Rom. 8:29*). The notion that because Christ has 'brothered' us, we may become children of God, lies at the heart of the New Testament's teaching about our salvation.

Considered from another perspective, we can say that bringing us into his family, making us children, is the work of the triune God in all his glory. The *Father* destines

[4]

us to be his children; the *Son* comes to make us his brothers and sisters; the *Spirit* is sent as the Spirit of adoption to make us fully aware of our privileges (*Rom. 8:15*). So, whether we view salvation from the standpoint of God its Author, or of Christians as we experience it, *sonship* is of central importance.

Our relationship with our heavenly Father has far-reaching practical implications for us as sons. It is by no means merely a matter of theoretical and speculative theology – an interesting idea, but practically irrelevant.

James I. Packer has written:

> You sum up the whole of the New Testament teaching in a single phrase, if you speak of it as a revelation of the Fatherhood of the holy Creator. In the same way, you sum up the whole of New Testament religion if you describe it as the knowledge of God as one's holy Father. If you want to judge how well a person understands Christianity, find out how much he makes of the thought of being God's child, and having God as his Father. If this is not the thought that prompts and controls his worship and prayers and his whole outlook on life, it means that he does not understand Christianity very well at all.[1]

This emphasis is an accurate assessment of the gospel. Of course, every area of biblical teaching and theology leads to its own practical implications. But the notion that we are children of God, his own sons and daughters, lies at the heart of all Christian theology, and is the mainspring of all Christian living.

Before we develop this thought further, we must first of all take time to review the biblical teaching that undergirds it. This we can do by emphasising the centrality of the idea of sonship.

[1] J. I. Packer, *Knowing God* (London: Hodder and Stoughton, 1973), p. 182.

How important is sonship in biblical teaching? We can express its centrality abruptly but truly by saying: *Our sonship to God is the apex of creation and the goal of redemption.*

God's first man was created as his image in order to be his son. Luke suggests that Adam was 'the son of God' in his genealogy of the Lord Jesus Christ (*Lk. 3:38*).

Looking to the future, we can see according to Scripture that the denouement of world history will be marked by the sons and daughters of God entering into the fullness of their liberty. Already predestined to be conformed to Christ so that he might be the firstborn in the family, they will enter into the fulness of their adoption at the resurrection (*Rom. 8:18–30*). This story of Paradise lost becoming Paradise regained is the story of God's grace bringing us from alienation from him to membership in his family. God's grace restores to us what Adam lost for us – sonship to the God who made us, loves us, and provides for us in every detail in life.

This focus on God's provision for us as his children unfolds itself in several ways in the course of biblical revelation.

First, it unfolds itself *in creation*. We noted that when God created man he made him to be his son (*Lk. 3:38*: 'Adam, the son of God'). To be a son, in the language of Genesis, was to be made in the image and likeness of one's father. So, when Seth was born to Adam and Eve, the event is recorded in these terms: 'When Adam had lived 130 years, he had a son in his own *likeness*, in his own *image*' (*Gen. 5:3*). Exactly the same phrase is used about the relationship between God and Adam. God made man in his *image* and *likeness* (*Gen. 1:26–27; 5:1–2*).

To be a son, and to be the image and likeness of your

father, are synonymous ideas. To put it another way, if we wish to understand what man was intended to be, we need to think of him as a son of God. If, in turn, we ask what it means to be a son of God, the answer must be found in terms of being God's image and likeness.

Few phrases in Scripture have proved to be more intriguing and apparently impenetrable than this. What does it mean to be the image and likeness of God? One clue is to be found in the fact that Christ himself, the Son of God incarnate, is described as being the image of God. By understanding what that means, we can begin to unravel what it means for us also to be God's image, since Christ came to restore to us the image that was marred through sin.

Christ came as the last Adam, the second man (*I Cor. 15:45–47*). In doing so, he took on himself three tasks. He was Prophet, Priest, and King. As the Christ (the Anointed One), he fulfilled in his life the roles that God had appointed in the Old Testament in order to give his people glimpses of what life in his kingdom was really all about. But, by fulfilling these roles, Christ was also demonstrating to us what God intended all his children to be.

God's sons were intended to be *prophets*, in the sense that they would speak God's word and reveal God's will to the created order. There is a hint of this in the creation narrative. There Adam names the animal kingdom, 'and whatever the man called each living creature, that was its name' (*Gen. 2:19*). *His* word was *God's* word to man's environment.

God's sons were also intended to be *priests*, expressing the praises and worship of the whole creation. At creation, all nature was made to unite in a magnificent symphony of worship to the Lord. But rational, articulate praise was expressed supremely by man as God's son. Man's voice and sacrifice of worship were significant to God because he was made as his image. Moreover, as God's son, in a special sense man was able to appreciate the sabbath day in which he could rest in the presence of his Father and enjoy worshipful contemplation of all the glories of creation (*Gen. 2:2–3*).

Then, thirdly, God's sons were created to be *kings* on the earth. In the complementary descriptions of creation in Genesis 1 and 2, man is presented as both the apex of creation (*Gen. 1*) and the centre of creation (*Gen. 2*). God gave him everything in the world as a gift ('I give you every seed-bearing plant on the face of the whole earth and every tree that has fruit with seed in it' (*Gen. 1:29*). He gave him dominion over the whole earth (*Gen. 1:26*). He was to be God's vice-gerent!

Man's life was that of a royal prince in the realm of his heavenly Father. The world was his principality – but one in which he was to demonstrate his loyalty in order to show himself capable of a richer degree of privilege and responsibility. Hence the command of God: 'You are free to eat from any tree in the garden; but you must not eat from the tree of the knowledge of good and evil, for when you eat of it you will surely die' (*Gen. 2:16–17*).

From this high dignity and these privileges, man fell. The image of God was fractured; the offices God gave to man were brought into disrepute as he disqualified himself from exercising them. True sonship to God thus became a memory of the past, a lost and unrecoverable privilege forfeited by sin.

Yet, in a sense, the image could still be seen, as Scripture elsewhere indicates (*Gen. 9:6, Jas. 3:9*). Because God remains man's Creator, man still retains indications that he was created to be God's son. But he is now God's image in the sense that a ruin is still a castle, or a palace. Its greatness lies in the past, in stark contrast to what it has become. Man is now by nature a great, but tragic figure. Like some character in a Shakespearean tragedy, he still stands on centre stage, but bears the marks of his own tragic destruction, rather than the glory of the image of God. Like the prodigal in the far country, he retains confused memories of his former family status, but feeds himself on the husks of a fallen world (*Lk. 15:14–16*).

God continues to unfold his love for his children in *restoration*. We have already seen the emphasis the New Testament in general places on the idea of sonship. Jesus' own preaching underscores what it means to be a child of the Father. In Paul's writings we find eloquent articulation of this concept against the background of the Old Testament revelation. He traces the Father's eternal purpose, the nature and function of Christ's incarnation, and the ministry of the Spirit, to this central fact – God is intent on restoring the image that he created of himself and his glory in the life of man.

Restoration of man to the image of God is an element in the gospel message that is frequently ignored in favour of other, equally biblical pictures of salvation like reconciliation, justification, and redemption. They are, however, its handmaidens. They describe various elements in God's ultimate purpose of restoration.

Such is the neglect of this emphasis that we sometimes find it difficult to appreciate the grandeur of the gospel. Thus, for example, when Paul speaks about *the world* being reconciled in Christ (*2 Cor. 5:19*), we feel a little ill at ease. We may lose sight of the breath-taking significance of this teaching because we instinctively interpret such statements in order to guard against the mistaken conclusion of universalism. But what Paul has in view in such passages (for example, *Eph. 1:9–10, Col. 1:19–20*) is the purpose of God to restore in his world the order and glory which had been there in the first place. The key to such restoration lies in the recovery of man to his original honour, dignity, privilege and responsibility. Reconciling all things to God, therefore, means fundamentally restoring to man the image that he reflected perfectly at creation but later marred by his sin.

Consequently, all our thinking about God's work should be organised around the principle he has enunciated in his word: 'Those God foreknew he also predestined to be conformed to the likeness of his Son, that he might be the firstborn among many brothers' (*Rom. 8:29*). God's final purpose is nothing less than a new race of men and women, restored to what they were intended to be, through their relationship to the divine image-bearer and Son, Jesus Christ.

Sonship, therefore, is everything! It is the goal of Christ's coming: 'But *when the time had fully come*, God sent his Son, born of a woman, born under law, to redeem those under law, *that we might receive the full rights of sons . . . So you are no longer a slave, but a son*; and *since you are a son*, God has made you also an heir' (*Gal. 4:4–7*).

Scripture also shows us the centrality of sonship in *redemption*. The manner of God's revelation in history and his working in our lives is consistent with this perspective. Precisely because God made us to be sons and intends to restore us to that status, the pattern of his working among his people reflects his ultimate goal. He means to bring many *sons* to glory (*Heb. 2:10*).

In the Old Testament the fundamental relationship between God and man was forged through God's covenant. He came to Noah, Abraham, Moses, and David and made his covenant with his people through them. He pledged himself to be their God, and to take them as his people. In that context, God gave himself to them *as a Father* and took his people to be his *children*. The language of the covenant is the language of the family. God's covenant people are his children, members of his family; he is their God and Father.

This pattern develops in redemptive history in three stages: in Israel, in Christ, and in us.

God took Israel, formed them into a people through the Exodus, and adopted them as his son. This is the great motif of the Exodus. Israel was God's firstborn among the nations of the world. Because Pharaoh sought to destroy Israel, God destroyed the firstborn of Pharaoh and his people and possessions: 'Then say to Pharaoh, "This is what the LORD says: Israel is *my firstborn son*, and I told you, 'Let my son go, so he may worship me.' But you refused to let him go; so I will kill your firstborn son"' (*Ex. 4:22–23*).

The Lord fulfilled his promise. His son, Israel, was set free: 'You saw how the LORD your God carried you, *as a father carries his son*, all the way you went until you reached this place' (*Deut. 1:31*). Subsequently, Moses was able to declare categorically to the people: 'You are *the children* of the LORD your God' (*Deut. 14:1*). But in due season God's children become unfaithful (*Deut. 32:20*). The Lord pleaded with his prodigal children through the ministry of the prophets, appealing to them: 'Hear, O heavens! Listen, O earth! For the LORD has spoken: "I reared children and brought them up, but they have rebelled against me. The ox knows his master, the donkey his owner's manger, but Israel does not know, my people do not understand"' (*Is. 1:2–3*). God laments the prodigality of his son: 'A son honours his father . . . If I am a father, where is the honour due me?' (*Mal. 1:6*). Malachi himself joined in the plea: 'Have we not all one Father? Did not one God create us? Why do we profane the covenant of our fathers by breaking faith with one another?' (*Mal. 2:10*).

The story of God's son Israel, of the 'adoption' which was his by grace (*Rom. 9:4*) is the story of a defection of unnatural proportions. The sonship that God restored in the choice and redemption of his people was despised. The birthright, the inheritance, was sold for a mess of pottage. Jacob became Israel; but in due season the people of Israel became the son of Jacob ('the clutcher').

Against this background the Sonship of Jesus Christ is revealed. He is the eternal Son of God. But he becomes a servant-Son in our flesh. He is all that Adam, and Israel after him, failed to be. This is one reason Paul calls him 'the second man' and 'the last Adam' (*1 Cor. 15:45–47*). He voluntarily makes his way into the far country of our prodigal sonship. He comes to us in our alienation from the Father, and by entering into our alienation ('My God, why have you forsaken me?' *Matt. 27:46*), he bestows on us a sonship that is ours by grace, not by nature.

★   ★   ★

Notice how Christ brings about our sonship. We have already seen that sonship to God was expressed in the role man had a prophet, priest, and king. Jesus, the One anointed with the Spirit without limit (*Jn. 3:34*), fulfils each of these offices. *As Prophet* he expresses and obeys the will of God (*Lk. 9:35; Heb. 1:1–2*); *as Priest* he renders praise to God in the one acceptable sacrifice of the cross (*Heb. 4:14–5:10; 8:1–2*); *as King* he rules – over himself, his enemies, and the world in which he lives (*Phil. 2:9–11*).

In Jesus the perfect image of God is seen once again – and in circumstances so different from those in which Adam sinned and fell. Christ is truly *the second man* – the only one to bear the image of God and to reflect God's intention for man since the fall. He is *the last Adam* – because he brings to consummation for us all that God commanded the first Adam to be. Jesus displays the image of God; Jesus shows us what true sonship means. In turn he becomes not only our Redeemer, but the great prototype of the work of God in all his children. We are his brothers, fellow-heirs with him (see *Heb. 2:5–18*). It should come as no surprise to us to learn that he is also the great blueprint for God's work in our lives. God intends to remake us into the likeness of our great Elder Brother. He is the firstborn of many brothers!

Enough has now been said to underline the fact that *sonship* is a fundamental thread in the weaving of God's plan. It is not the only thread, but it is a vital one.

*　　*　　*

Sonship carries important practical implications for our Christian lives. One of the most fundamental is illustrated in Jesus' parable of the prodigal son. Undoubtedly this parable should be called the parable of the two sons, or even of the elder brother. The context makes that clear (*Lk. 15:1–2*). The elder brother represents a Pharisee. But this Pharisee lurks in the hearts of most men, and his influence may not be wholly destroyed by conversion.

The elder brother lived with the father; he served the father – indeed (as the NIV vividly translates) he felt he had '*slaved*' for the father (*Lk. 15:29*). It was ultimately the elder brother who proved to be in the far country, spiritually. He had never entered into a true filial relationship with his father. He thought of his father as a slave-master, and himself as a slave, not as a son.

Many Christians retain some measure of the spirit of the elder brother. They remain at a distance from God; they may even regard obedience in the Christian life as a form of slavery. Emotionally and psychologically their view of God's gracious purpose is warped and yields reluctantly to the influences of God's word. Suspicion of the Father is more characteristic of them than enjoying fellowship with him. They cannot trust him, and so they do not know the joy of self-abandonment to him as their Father in heaven. *They experience only what Paul calls 'a spirit that makes you a slave' (Rom. 8:15).*

The Christian church is plagued today, perhaps even more than in other times, with slick and immediate answers to such spiritual difficulties. But what is really needed is a biblical answer, precisely because these are theological as well as emotional or psychological problems. For their root lies in our idea of God, and how we think of our relationship to him. No short-cut that tries to bypass the patient unfolding of the true character of God, and our relationship to him as his children, can ever succeed in providing long-term spiritual therapy. But the knowledge that the Father has bestowed his love on us, so that we are called children of God – and in fact *are* his children (*1 Jn. 3:1–2*), will, over time, prove to be the solvent in which our fears, mistrust, and suspicion of God – as well as our sense of distance from him – will eventually dissolve. Then we will enter into a richer experience of confidence and assurance as the children of our Father in heaven.

The following chapters explore this confidence and assurance in a variety of areas of key biblical teaching on the Christian as a child of the living God.

2
New
Birth

God's ultimate purpose is to honour his Son, Jesus Christ, by making him the 'firstborn of many brothers' (*Rom. 8:29*). He intends to make us children of God. But, how does he accomplish this?

Even to put the question in this form is to deny a commonly held opinion: namely, that we are all, naturally, God's children. But, did not Jesus teach his disciples to call God 'Father'? Did not Paul agree that we are all God's 'offspring' (*Acts 17:28*)?

In the sense that God is the Creator of all things, it is true that the Bible sometimes speaks of his Fatherhood. He is the 'Father of the heavenly lights' (*Jas. 1:17*) and the One who brought the universe to birth. But that is not the most common usage of the idea of God's Fatherhood in Scripture. Normally it is limited to the special Father–Son relationship that exists between God the Father and his Son, Jesus Christ, and also between God the Father and those who know and trust him. Indeed, since the idea of God's Fatherhood implies our sonship and *fellowship* with him, it is rather obvious that not all men and women are his children or call him Father.

This is a basic assumption of the Christian gospel: we are not, by nature, children of God. We need to *become* his children. By nature we are alienated from God. Such is the burden of Paul's argument in Romans 1:18–3:20. Not one of us possesses, by nature, the characteristics of a child of God. Instead, we show all the signs of rebelling against him and turning away from his Fatherly rule over our lives. We do not know what it means to be at peace with him (*Rom. 3:17*); we do not know what it is to have a filial fear of him (*Rom. 3:18*). This is why the gospel is so necessary for us.

In fact, by nature, we are children of wrath, not children of God (*Eph. 2:3*, where the NIV word 'objects' is, literally, 'children', *tekna*). Rather than seeing us as amiable mischiefs, God sees us as we really are in his sight – unfaithful sinners worthy only of his judgment, 'prodigal sons' who are both 'lost' and 'dead' (*Lk. 15:31*). There could be no more serious delusion for us to suffer from, therefore, than that we are naturally his children. Rather, we need to *become* children of God.

All this is assumed in the Prologue to John's Gospel when he says: 'To all who received him, to those who believed in his name, he gave the right to become children of God – children born not of natural descent, nor of human decision or a husband's will, but born of God' (*Jn. 1:12–13*). He could not be more unequivocal; we need to *become* God's children. Moreover, we can become his children only *by the decision of God's will*. The new birth of which John speaks here and elsewhere is not ours by nature, nor is it within our natural powers to accomplish! Not only is this devastating to human pride, but it also underlines the spiritual peril of our natural condition.

The Prologue to John's Gospel serves the same function as the overture does in a symphony. It suggests the various motifs which are to be more fully worked out in what follows. John explains and illustrates what he means by this birth from God when, later, in Chapter 3, he describes the encounter between Jesus and Nicodemus.

Nicodemus was 'Israel's teacher', and yet he did not seem able to understand our Lord's teaching on the necessity of the new birth for all those who would become children of God (*Jn. 3:10*). Here was a man with every possible natural advantage: a Jew, with the promises and word of God at his fingertips; a Pharisee, living scrupulously close to the law of God; a student of theology – more, the leading professor of theology among his peers. Nicodemus was a religious devotee, if ever there was one. Yet he did not understand that he needed to be born again in order to become a child of God and enter his kingdom.

Nicodemus illustrates all that it is possible to be without being a member of the family of God. When Jesus told him that no one can either see or enter God's kingdom without being born again, Nicodemus illustrated the very failure to see the kingdom of which Jesus spoke. 'How can this be?' (*Jn. 3:9*) he asked. Only later would he understand the difference between belonging to the family of God and being a member of the family of the devil (cf. *Jn. 8:42–47; 19:39, 1 Jn. 3:10*).

What, then, is this new birth of which Jesus spoke, which lies at the heart of belonging to God's family? It has often been understood to be a special, personal, conversion experience. In recent years it almost became fashionable to be 'born again'; it was described by the media as a sociological 'movement'. But very often the phrase denoted little more than having a religious experience of the vaguest kind. The New Testament means something much more specific.

Here it is important to enter a word of caution. 'Born again' and 'regeneration' can very easily become 'buzz words'. But using biblical language does not mean we have had genuine biblical experience. A little knowledge of the New Testament's background would help us to understand that. The idea of regeneration or new birth was not limited to the Christian faith in the first century AD. On the contrary, it was commonplace among the mystery religions of the ancient world. (That may be the reason why Paul generally avoids this terminology.) Hence the New Testament places considerable stress on explaining what it means when it speaks of being 'born again'. In a nutshell, it means *to come to share in the risen life and power of Jesus Christ, and to enter into vital fellowship with him.*

Jesus prophesied that a final 'new birth' or 'regeneration' would take place at the end of time (*Matt. 19:28*). His resurrection from the dead was actually the firstfruits of that great event (*1 Cor. 15:20*). By it he became 'the firstborn of many brothers'. God's ultimate purpose is to conform us to the image of his Son in the same way, through our resurrection (*Phil. 3:21*).

In this sense, we can rightly speak about Jesus' resurrection as his 'new birth'. He was dead because of sin (ours, not his). But God raised him into new life (*Rom. 6:9–10*). He was transformed and marked out as the Son of God with power through the resurrection (*Rom. 1:3–4*), and thus entered into a new dimension of humanity altogether, in which 'death no longer has mastery over him' (*Rom. 6:9*).

Consequently, Paul could speak of the resurrection of Jesus as the day on which he was 'born' into the new family of God:

We tell you the good news: What God promised our fathers he has fulfilled for us, their children, by raising up Jesus. As it is written in the second Psalm: 'You are my Son; today I have become your Father' (*Acts 13:32*).

Paul saw that the 'today' of Psalm 2 was pointing to the resurrection of Jesus. That did not mean that Jesus 'became' God's Son at the resurrection. It meant that as the God-man, the 'man for others', he took the first steps of man on the ground of the world to come. In a far more profound sense than Neil Armstrong's words, when he took the very first step made by man on the Moon, the morning of the resurrection of Jesus was 'a giant leap for mankind'. For what took place in the Elder Brother will one day take place in the lives of all the children. Not only so, but *already*, through fellowship with him in our regeneration, through 'new birth', we experience the first rays of that glorious morning. The light of the world to come has already crept over the horizon of our lives and is shining into the death-darkened days in which we live (*Rom. 13:11–12*).

This birth of a new brotherhood sheds light on the otherwise enigmatic words of Jesus to Mary Magdalene on the morning of the resurrection. As she clung to him, Jesus said, 'Do not hold on to me, for I have not yet returned to the Father. Go instead to my brothers and tell them, "I am returning to my Father and your Father, to my God and your God"' (*Jn. 20:17*).

These words are usually understood to draw a distinction between Jesus' relationship to the Father and that which his disciples were to enjoy. In fact their purpose is to teach almost the reverse! Jesus is saying: 'Just as in the resurrection, God has brought me to new birth, so by your spiritual resurrection you have come to share with me in fellowship with him. He is my Father, but since you are my brothers he is also your Father, in the family of God.'

Paul makes essentially the same point when he describes God's work of grace in Christ as a 'new creation' (*2 Cor. 5:17*). God brought creation into being for his glory, and to be the sphere of man's life as God's son. He made man (that is, man and woman) as his image (*Gen. 1:26–27*). In the world of the Old Testament, as we have already seen, the idea of bearing someone's 'image' is related to family-likeness (cf. *Gen. 5:3*).

At creation man was made as the image of God, or as the son of God. But he has fallen from that status. The glory for which he was made has been profoundly marred and its reality distorted. The whole creation has been tragic-ally affected – so much so that Paul says that 'the whole creation has been groaning as in the pains of childbirth right up to the present time' (*Rom. 8:22*). But what birth is creation expecting? Paul has already explained: 'The creation was subjected to frustration, not by its own choice, but by the will of the one who subjected it, in hope that the creation itself will be liberated from its bondage to decay and brought into the glorious freedom of the children of God' (*Rom. 8:20–21*).

Scripture looks forward to a day when all that was originally meant to be will come to pass. The fall of man, with its accompanying frustration and decay in the natural order, will be rectified. There will be a new creation in which the entire universe will participate. This is what Paul means when he speaks of the new creation. Then, all that God intended men and women to be as his image, as his sons and daughters, will be fulfilled. This is what Jesus described as 'the regeneration' (*Matt. 19:28*, A.V.). It will be a new creation.

But this is not simply some '*far off* divine event to which the whole creation moves' (Tennyson). From the New Testament's point of view, there are signs that it has *already* begun. Jesus' resurrection was the beginning of this new creation. He is the first sign of God's *springtime*, and the guarantee of the *final harvest*. The 'regeneration' has already begun with him. It continues with each of us when we are united to him by God's grace, and share in the new family of which he is the 'firstborn' (*Col. 1:18*, *Heb. 12:23*). To become a child of God, to be 'born again', therefore, involves nothing less than sharing in the risen life and brotherhood of Jesus!

In our present time we need to learn to appreciate the magnitude of our relationship with Jesus, for several reasons.

One is that we have a tendency to think of being 'born again' as an inexplicable, private, mystical 'experience'. For the New Testament, however, being born again meant entering into fellowship and brotherhood with Jesus Christ. (This is why the teaching on new birth in John 3 is set in the context of instruction about trusting in and believing on Jesus as Saviour, *Jn. 3:16*).

A second reason for emphasising our new brotherhood with Jesus is that it helps us to see what a glorious thing the new birth is. We tend to have a very superficial appreciation of what God has done for us. When it dawns on us that we have entered into brotherhood with the risen Lord Jesus Christ, that we now participate in the power of his resurrection, that the glory of God's image is being restored in our lives – then everyone who has been born again will rejoice in the grandeur of the change that God has accomplished in us through his Spirit! We will not (as some mistakenly do) wish we had a more spectacular 'experience of conversion', because we will realise that the grace of God is just as wonderful in our lives as in the lives of those whose conversions make headline news in the Christian media. It is no easier for God to give *you* a new birth than it is for him to give it to the worst man who ever lived!

In Chapter Four we will notice some of the effects of regeneration in the life of the Christian. But at this juncture we should underline an important statement from Paul's teaching. Speaking of what is involved in regeneration as it is symbolised by baptism, Paul says that believers have been 'united with him [Christ] in his death' and 'we will certainly also be united with him in his resurrection' (*Rom. 6:5*).

The expression 'united with' is a very interesting word in Paul's vocabulary. It may be derived either from the verb 'to plant together with', or 'to grow together with'. Scholars are not in agreement. But in either case it provides a vivid picture of becoming a Christian through rebirth. It means to be planted with Jesus in the soil of his death to sin, *or*, to be united with Jesus in such a way that our Christian lives grow in union with him in his death to sin (*Rom. 6:10*: 'The death he died, he died to sin'). Paul further emphasises this sense when he writes that we are (literally) *the kind of people* who 'died to sin' (*Rom. 6:2*).

What does this dying to sin mean? From the moment of rebirth we enter into a changed relationship with the sin that once held us captive. We 'died' to it. It is no longer our master, and we are no longer its slave. Formerly, it reigned over us, ruled us like a general would direct the artillery at his disposal, and, as our employer, paid us wages (see *Rom. 6:14,17,23*, for these word-pictures).

Paul does not mean that we are totally free from the presence or influence of sin. Sin still indwells the children of God (*Rom. 7:17, 20*), but they no longer have the same relationship to it. They belong to a new family in which sin is not 'the order of the day'. Instead, righteousness, peace, and joy mark the family life of God's people (*Rom. 14:17*). We are 'the kind of people' who have begun to taste that deliverance from the reign of sin, which will be consummated at the regeneration of all things.

How helpful this teaching should be to us in an age when so many people have lost their sense of identity, and search either for roots in the past, or somewhere they can belong in the present. Our roots are in Jesus Christ; we belong to him and his family. We have a new strength and security built into our way of life because of regeneration.

How, then, does regeneration take place? Like natural birth, it is not something we ourselves instigate. By nature we are dead in transgressions and sins (*Eph. 2:1*). God alone is able to bring us to new birth, through the Spirit. He does so through the power of Christ's resurrection from the dead (*1 Pet. 1:3*). Just as Christ stood at the tomb of Lazarus and called his name, and the dead man came to life and emerged from the tomb (*Jn. 11:43–44*), so Jesus Christ speaks into the death of our hearts, calls us by name, and we respond (*Jn. 5:25; 10:3*). As at the first creation, so in the new creation God breathes on us with his Spirit, and we are brought into new life. Regeneration is a sovereign act of God.

But like natural birth, in which we are unconscious of the precise moment of our conception, yet active in coming from our mother's womb and giving our first cry of life, so it is in regeneration. Given new life by God, we too cry out. But our cry, Paul tells us – significantly in his great chapter on sonship – is '*Abba*, Father' (*Rom. 8:15*). This, perhaps more than anything else, is the sign that we have been 'born again'. We have come to know God *as our Father*. This is the beginning of a new life which will develop more and more in the disciplines, service, privileges, and joys of the family of God.

With such a life in prospect, who would remain content until he had been born into such a family?

3
Adopted Children

We have seen that we become children of our heavenly Father through the Holy Spirit's power in bringing us into new life in Christ. He gives us new birth. A *creative* act of God takes place, by which we are brought into a new family. We become children in the kingdom of God.

There is another dimension to our sonship that we should consider. In the world of the Bible, sonship was a legal, as well as a created, relationship. A son was recognised as such by a definite act on his father's part. Thus, for example, it seems to have been the traditional way of accepting a child as one's own when the child was actually born on the knees of the father, or placed on the knees of the one who was to be regarded as the father (for an example of this, see *Gen. 50:23*).

In the New Testament's understanding of the Christian as a child of God, this same dual dimension exists. We are born into God's family through the work of the Spirit. But we are also brought into that family by a decisive, legal act on God's part. The apostle Paul thought this latter dimension illuminated Christian experience, and he used the concept of *adoption* (*huiothesia* – to be placed as a son) to describe it.

Biblical scholars have long researched the source of this idea in Paul's writings. Many of them have concluded that the Old Testament does not really employ the concept of adoption. Old Testament family life was so structured that 'adoption' was unnecessary. On the other hand, the Hellenistic world in which Paul moved, governed by Roman law, did have such a concept. So, it has been argued that the background to Paul's description of Christians as God's adopted children is to be found in the Roman legal system.

Paul did not shape the gospel to suit the secular world of his time. It would be mistaken, therefore, to think that he took the Roman legal concept and moulded the message of the gospel into it. Rather, he saw that the Roman concept of adoption does provide a valuable way of describing the Christian's sonship. As Professor Francis Lyall has written:

> The profound truth of Roman adoption was that the adoptee was taken out of his previous state and was placed in a new relationship of son to his new father, his new *paterfamilias* [head of the household]. All his old debts are cancelled, and in effect the adoptee started a new life as part of his new family. From that time on the *paterfamilias* had the same control over his new 'child' as he had over his natural offspring. He owned all the property and acquisitions of the adoptee, controlled his personal relationships, and had rights of discipline. On the other hand the father was liable for the actions of the adoptee, and each owed the other reciprocal duties of support and maintenance.[1]

This Roman background seems to be confirmed by the fact that the only occasions on which Paul uses the

[1]Francis Lyall, *Slaves, Citizens, Sons: Legal Metaphors in the Epistles* (Grand Rapids: Zondervan, 1984), p. 83.

expression 'adopted son' (*huiothesia*) are in the letters he wrote to the churches in Rome or in Roman colonies (*Rom. 8:15; 9:4, Gal.4:5, Eph. 1:5*).

There are, then, two dimensions to our sonship. The first is re-creation (or regeneration); the second is adoption, God's acceptance of us into his family. This second element is what we must now examine in a little more detail.

The source of adoption is to be found in God. Just as we were born again of his will (*Jas. 1:18*), so we are adopted because of his love. This is the reason John assigns for our status as sons: 'How great is the love the Father has lavished on us, that we should be called children of God!' (*1 Jn. 3:1*). The word John uses, *potapos*, means 'of what kind'. Here it may have the meaning, 'of what a size!' In fact *potapos* is from the earlier classical Greek *podapos*, which means 'from what country'. Perhaps that captures John's meaning – he is talking about a love that belongs to another country, or world altogether! In any case John's sense of astonishment is obvious. He places full emphasis on the 'us' who are the objects of God's love. He means those who had abandoned God and his will, who had despised his providence and love. It is almost incredible that God should make *us* his children!

Think for a moment about the situation of the prodigal son as he contemplated returning home to his father. The thought uppermost in his mind was this: 'How many of my father's hired men have food to spare, and here I am starving to death! I will set out and go back to my father and say to him: Father, I have sinned against heaven and against you. I am no longer worthy to be called your son; make me like one of your hired men' (*Lk. 15:17–19*).

He was, of course, quite right. He had already received his birthright. He had already destroyed all that was legally his as a son by demanding and then squandering his share of the inheritance. He spoke the simple truth when he said he was no longer worthy to be called his father's son.

But, inevitably, the guilt-ridden son was calculating on the basis of his sin, rather than on the basis of his father's character. For, when he returned, he experienced what John describes in his letter – the love that a father lavishes on his children.

No doubt, at first, the prodigal boy did not believe what was happening. There was his father, running, throwing his arms around his wayward child, embracing him, 'filled with compassion for him' as Jesus says. But the son's heart was probably still saying: 'I have sinned against heaven and against you. I am no longer worthy to be called your son.' His sin had so burdened him with guilt that he just could not have expected his father's loving gestures. How could his father still love him? In response his father demonstrated his love by giving him the best robe, the ring, and the celebration party.

Although this story is probably the best known and loved of all Christ's parables, the lesson it teaches us *as Christians* is often overlooked. Jesus was underlining the fact that – despite assumptions to the contrary – the reality of the love of God for us is often the last thing in the world to dawn upon us. As we fix our eyes upon ourselves, our past failures, our present guilt, it seems impossible to us that the Father could love us.

Many Christians go through much of their life with the prodigal's suspicion. Their concentration is upon their sin and failure; all their thoughts are introspective. That is why (in the Greek text) John's statement about the Father's love begins with a word calling us to lift up our eyes from ourselves and take a long look at what God has done: *Behold!* – look and see – the love the Father has lavished upon us!

The parable in fact sheds even more light upon this phenomenon. For it is commonly held that the Fatherhood of God and the brotherhood of men are truths of which men are instinctively aware. But the very opposite is the case. By instinct men without Christ do not believe that the Father loves them. On the contrary, they are like the elder brother; they believe that God is a hard and demanding taskmaster. They react antagonistically to the demonstration the Father has given of his unearned and demerited grace.

This failure to recognise the Father's graciousness is precisely what we see in our Lord's description of the elder brother in the parable. He was geographically near to his father, but spiritually he was the one who lived in 'the far country', alienated from his father's love and grace. Ultimately it was he, and not the younger son, who 'refused to go in'. He refused to believe that the father really loved him. Rather, his attitude was (as the NIV perfectly expresses it): 'Look! All these years I've been slaving for you and never disobeyed your orders' (*Lk. 15:29*). He had never known inwardly what it meant to be a son at all!

Contrast, then, these two attitudes:

(1) '*Look!* All these years I've been slaving for you and never disobeyed your orders' (*Lk. 15:29*); or,

(2) *Look!* 'How great is the love the Father has lavished on us that we should be called children of God!' (*1 Jn. 3:1*).

Which of them is more appropriate to your spiritual condition?

John Cotton, one of the most influential preachers among the founding fathers of New England, quaintly expressed the same point when he wrote in his own exposition of the word 'Behold' in 1 John 3:1 (A.V.):

This reproves men's squint looking. They do not look at

God's love, but at themselves and at their own corruptions and afflictions. It is a wonder that God's children should pore only upon their corruptions, and not consider what love it is for God to discover them and pardon them.[2]

Similarly, John Owen, a contemporary of Cotton, and a man greatly influenced by his teaching, noticed how even Christians tend to look at the Father 'with . . . anxious, doubtful thoughts. . . . What fears, what questionings are there, of his good-will and kindness! At the best, many think there is no sweetness at all in him towards us, but what is purchased at the high price of the blood of Jesus.'[3]

The trend of religious and evangelical thought today is the reverse. We have recently come through the era in which the great motto of multitudes of Christians has been: 'Smile, God loves you!' But such buttons and bumper stickers can sometimes be a substitute for the reality they proclaim! They cannot give a deep inward persuasion that God does love us, and a knowledge of how that love is manifested to us in calling us his children. By contrast the knowledge of our adoption does something theologically, spiritually, and psychologically for us which all the lapel buttons in the world can never achieve!

*   *   *

In keeping with the Roman concept of adoption, Paul's teaching meant basically three things: the old family ties were broken; a new family was joined; and new

[2]John Cotton, *Commentary on 1 John, ad. 3:1.*
[3]John Owen, *Communion with God* (1657) in *The Works of John Owen*, ed. W. H. Goold, volume II (reprinted London: Banner of Truth Trust, 1966), p. 32.

commitments were made on the part of that new family.
These same elements are involved in our adoption into the
family of God.

THE OLD FAMILY TIES ARE BROKEN

We were children of wrath, servants and slaves in the
kingdom of darkness. We were separated from God and
his family. But we are so 'no longer'. Now we are
'members of God's household' (*Eph. 2:3, 12, 19*).

Our adoption into God's family implies that all of our
old obligations and debts are cancelled. We are no longer
legally bound to the burden of guilt or the sinful way of life
that characterised us before we became Christians (*Rom.
6:17–18*).

We have already seen, in the illustration of the prodigal
son, that Christians often find it difficult to believe that
God's unfailing love is real. This is where the knowledge
and increasing assurance that we are children of God is a
refuge and shield against the attacks of Satan. Just as part
of his plan of action in his temptation of Jesus included the
issue of whether he was really the Son of God (compare
Matt. 4:3, 6), so a parallel issue arises with us. Satan will
cast up to us the sins of both the past and the present; he
will allure us with temptations to sin to which we may fall
in the future, and then lead us to question the reality of our
relationship to God. Can we be God's children after all,
when such thoughts lurk in our minds, and such deeds lie
in our past?

What is the answer to this kind of temptation? It is, at
least in part, the recollection that we are not children of
God by worth and merit, but by free, gracious adoption.
God has chosen us. Our status is not a matter of our
worthiness, but of his love!

When the elder brother in the parable complained, he

suggested that the younger brother was a hypocrite in accepting the father's lavish love, because he had 'squandered your property with prostitutes' (notice the possible exaggeration, characteristic of Satan-inspired doubts and innuendos!). The father's answer does not justify this receiving of God's grace, however, but points out that it was *need, not merit*, that received compassion and salvation. That is why we no longer bear the burden of our past lives.

How can it be that we are free of this burden? It is because we are adopted *in Christ*. Just as we saw that regeneration is a sharing in Christ's resurrection, there is also a sense in which adoption is sharing in Christ's adoption as Son of God with power in the resurrection. For the resurrection is not only an act of divine power in Jesus' life; it is a declaration of legal adoption (*Rom. 1:4*). The resurrection is the legal demonstration that the Son – who was not spared on the cross but died there under the divine judgement, experiencing the depths of separation from God, crying out: 'My God, my God, why have you forsaken me?' – has been welcomed into God's family afresh as his Son. The Son of God, who went into the far country for our sake, has returned from death and has been welcomed by the Father! By God's grace, we share that welcome!

When we say that our adoption means that all our debts and obligations are cancelled, we do not mean that they have simply been nullified by divine *fiat*. Rather, they were put to the account of God's Son. He took the bill of debt to the cross and nailed it there (*Col. 2:14*). His death wrote the word 'cancelled' over all our debts. So when we are adopted into God's family, it is only *through Christ*, and *at infinite cost to him*. This is what John has in mind when he tells us to fix our minds on the greatness of the love that God has lavished on us, since it was while we were weak,

[31]

sinful, and without strength that Christ died for us (*Rom. 5:6, 8–10*). He died, the just for the unjust, to bring us to God and to introduce us into his family as his adopted children. All past debts and ties are now cancelled. Having been put to his account, they have been paid by Christ on our behalf.

THE NEW FAMILY PRIVILEGES BECOME OURS

Becoming a child of God brings with it a host of privileges to which we will give consideration in later chapters. For the moment, however, several should be mentioned.

First, *Jesus Christ is not ashamed to have us as his brothers!* (*Heb. 2:11*). What do we have in common with him? By nature we are a disgrace to him, a cause of shame. He perfectly mirrors the image and glory of God; we have spoiled it. He served his Father with joyful obedience; we have rebelled against his will. He loved the Father; we have spurned him. It is inconceivable that we should have anything in common. Yet the writer of Hebrews indicates what Christ did in order to enter into a relationship of fellowship with us of which he would not be ashamed. He took our nature, our humanity, and in it destroyed the powers that have rendered us objects of shame in the sight of the glorious God. He who is holy, and makes us holy by his grace, brings us into his own family. Because he has cleansed and sanctified us, he is not ashamed of us (*Heb. 2:10–11*). We are *his brothers!* What a motivation that is to live like the brothers of Jesus Christ and the children of the living God!

A second privilege is, *as sons, we have the privilege of calling God, 'Abba, Father.'*

The late New Testament scholar Joachim Jeremias gave considerable attention to the phenomenon that, in Judaism, men rarely, if ever, prayed to God as 'Father'.

They certainly did not normally talk to him using the intimate, affectionate term 'Abba'. Jeremias concluded that in this word we have the repetition by the church of the way in which the Lord Jesus himself normally addressed God (cf. *Mk. 14:36* with *Rom. 8:15* and *Gal. 4:6*).[4] The unique, intimate relationship between the Father and the Son was now being shared by the Son with all his people! This privilege Jesus himself described:

> All things have been committed to me by my Father. No-one knows the Son except the Father, and no-one knows the Father except the Son *and those to whom the Son chooses to reveal him (Matt. 11:27).*

If you are a son of God, by grace, you may call him 'Abba, Father'.

It is always a moving privilege when someone whom you admire takes you aside and says: 'I would appreciate it if you would no longer call me "Mr." but simply "John".' But that privilege pales into insignificance by comparison with what we have here. Christ is giving us access to the presence of his Father, and saying to us: 'You may now speak to him as I speak to him; with the same right of access, with the same sense of intimacy, with the same assurance that he loves you.' This is, of course, what Jesus means when he tells us, 'Pray in my name' (*Jn. 14:13–14; 15:16; 16:23–26*). He does not merely mean that our prayers should conclude with the formula 'in Jesus' name'. He means that we may speak with the Father just as he speaks with the Father, for the Father's ear will open as readily to our cries as it does to the voice of his own Son.

A third privilege of God's children is, *as sons, we are recipients of the Father's tender care, and the compassion of our Elder Brother*. Elements of this were already present in the

---

[4]Joachim Jeremias, *The Prayers of Jesus* (London: S.C.M. Press, 1967), p. 65.

revelation of God's character in the Old Testament: 'As a
father has compassion on his children, so the LORD has
compassion on those who fear him' (*Ps. 103:13*). To his
rebellious son Israel, God speaks through Hosea:

> When Israel was a child, I loved him,
>   and out of Egypt I called my son.
> But the more I called Israel,
>   the further they went from me . . .
>
> How can I give you up, Ephraim?
>   How can I hand you over, Israel?
> How can I treat you like Admah?
>   How can I make you like Zeboiim?
> My heart is changed within me;
>   all my compassion is aroused.
>
> (*Hosea 11:1–2, 8*)

Nowhere is God's unfailing love more movingly por-
trayed than in Ezekiel's allegory of Jerusalem's unfaith-
fulness, in a passage that comes closer than possibly any
other to the idea that God had adopted Israel to be his
own:

> Your ancestry and birth were in the land of the
> Canaanites; your father was an Amorite and your
> mother a Hittite. On the day you were born your cord
> was not cut, nor were you washed with water to make
> you clean, nor were you rubbed with salt or wrapped in
> cloth. No-one looked on you with pity or had compas-
> sion enough to do any of these things for you. Rather,
> you were thrown out into the open field, for on the day
> you were born you were despised.
>   Then I passed by and saw you kicking about in your
> blood, and as you lay there in your blood I said to you,
> 'Live!' I made you grow like a plant of the field . . .
>   Later I passed by, and when I looked at you and saw
> that you were old enough for love, I spread the corner of
> my garment over you, and covered your nakedness. I

gave you my solemn oath and entered into a covenant with you, declares the Sovereign LORD, and you became mine (*Ez. 16:3–8*).

But it is in Christ that we see this compassion of the Father expressed most fully. Such is his concern for his brothers that he comes to enter into the heart of their weakness and frailty, temptations and fears. He calls us his brothers and tells us that he sympathises with us. But more than that, he actually enters into our flesh in his incarnate ministry, and feels with us, as he experiences what we experience. So the author of the letter to the Hebrews is able to say: 'We have one who has been tempted in every way, *just as we are* – yet was without sin' (*Heb. 4:15*). As a tempted brother, he feels for us; as a sinless brother he can save us.

The Gospels portray what this identification meant in Jesus' life in very moving, practical terms. *He touched lepers*, thereby endangering his own flesh, and placing himself under the same legal judgement they experienced. *He shared the table of sinners*, emphasising that he had come to have fellowship with them in order that they might be raised to have fellowship with him. *He wept and groaned; he tasted human weakness and fear.* ('Never man feared like this Man,' said Martin Luther of our Lord Jesus' loud crying and tears in the Garden of Gethsemane.) *He was bewildered* by what God was doing in his life ('My God, *why* have you forsaken me?' *Matt. 27:46*). His sympathy is not merely verbal, therefore, or theoretical. It is actual, and real. For he is indeed our Brother Saviour, our Kinsman Redeemer.

In the course of the Sermon on the Mount, Jesus said that this same compassionate caring is true of his Father. 'Your Father knows what you need,' before you ask' (*Matt. 6:8*). Here is strong reassurance for us: God knows,

[35]

and he is my Father. I am entitled to use the argument Jesus taught me to use: if I, as an earthly (and sinful) parent, know how to give good gifts to my children, how much more will the heavenly Father give good gifts to those who are his children? (see *Matt. 7:9–11*). The logic is irrefutable. The argument should be conclusive: he is my Father; I am his child. I (who am sinful) care for my own children, and long for their blessing. *How much more*, then, will my (perfect) heavenly Father care for me!

We need to learn this strong biblical logic, if we are to overcome the doubts of our hearts and the insinuations of the Evil One. Only as I begin to think along these lines will I come to an assured sense that my life and the lives of my fellow Christians, my spiritual family, are secure in the hands of the Father. After all, he is 'the Father of the heavenly lights, who does not change like shifting shadows'. It is he who 'chose to give us birth through the word of truth, that we might be a kind of firstfruits of all he created' (*Jas. 1:17–18*).

THREE VITAL IMPLICATIONS

In thinking about our adoption as children of God, there are three final implications of the New Testament's teaching we need to appreciate.

First, *adoption is not a change in nature, but a change in status*. If we fail to see this truth, we will miss the significance of our adoption. Similarly, if we think of adoption as based on anything we have done, or on what we are, then we will jeopardise our assurance of God's Fatherly relation to us. Adoption is, instead, *a declaration God makes about us*. It is irreversible, dependent entirely upon his gracious choice, in which he says: 'You are my son, today I have brought you into my family.'

As we look at ourselves, we may not see perfect signs of that family relationship in our lives. We may be tempted to despair that we will ever live worthily of this wonderful calling. But our assurance of our relationship to God does not lie in ourselves, but in the fact that through faith in Christ we have become sons of God (*Gal. 3:26*). We are adopted into God's family by the resurrection of Christ from the death in which he paid all our obligations to sin, the law, and the devil, in whose family we once lived. Our old status lies in his tomb.[5] A new status is ours through his resurrection.

Secondly, *adoption into a new family produces conflict with the old family*. From time to time, situations appear in the news media in which a child has been adopted – and the original parent or parents seek to have the child who is naturally theirs restored to their home. The adoption intended to bring security to the child can now only do so if the demands of the old family are resisted. Yet, perhaps, the child has an ingrained sense that it is the old family, not the new, to which he naturally belongs. He or she feels pulled in two opposite directions. But the issue should not be in doubt. The new family has legal rights, the former family has none.

How like the experience of the Christian! Satan endeavours to win us back. He slanders the treatment we receive at the hands of our new Father. He says: 'Look at the difficulties, trials, and sufferings you have experienced since you joined the Christian family – God doesn't *really* love you! Look at the way you no longer enjoy the things you used to enjoy . . . at first you felt a great sense of relief as you quietened your conscience by deciding to follow

[5]There is no more graphic illustration of this in English literature than in John Bunyan's classic description of the Christian life, *The Pilgrim's Progress*. When Christian is forgiven at the Cross of Christ, the burden of his past guilt rolls away *into the tomb*, to lie buried there!

Christ . . . but imagine how much you have lost by doing that . . . look at what your old friends are enjoying . . . look how less demanding life is for them than it is for you . . . You simply can't keep up these standards . . . and you would be a hypocrite if you gave the impression you were *really* wanting to.' But we need not fear. His desperate attacks underline that we no longer belong to his kingdom. He wants to win us back only because he knows he has lost us (cf. *Rev. 12:12*).

We should remember that Satan's attacks are a characteristic of the Christian life. There is conflict because we are in a new family!

A third implication of the New Testament's teaching is that *adoption is incomplete in this world*. John says that we are *called* God's children; he adds that we *are* God's children; but it does *not yet* appear what we *shall be* in the future, when Christ appears and we are made like him (*1 Jn. 3:1–3*). Similarly Paul teaches us that although we have already received the Spirit of adoption, and cry 'Abba, Father' (*Rom. 8:15*), we are still waiting for the full experience of our sonship, for 'the glorious freedom of the children of God' (*Rom. 8:21*). The redemption of our bodies, our adoption in all its glory, takes place finally at the resurrection. Then, the seed that has been sown will blossom; the image now under repair will be completed. Then we will experience adoption in a measure we do not now understand.

Adoption assures us that we have a new status. But because it also involves us in the most serious of 'family feuds', it serves as a reminder that God has still more to show us of his grace and power.

In the light of this reminder we need to learn that while adoption offers us glorious privileges, a minor key runs through the melody of our present lives. We must take note of that minor key and know why it is there.

Otherwise we will readily fall prey to the insinuations springing from Satan, the world, and our own weak, doubting spirits, that the Christian life is not all we expected it would be.

At the moment, as adopted sons and daughters, we are heirs. We experience our inheritance in part. The day will dawn when we experience it fully. Already we have experienced much; but there is to be more. For the moment, then, let us trust in the wisdom of our Father in heaven who knows and supplies all we shall ever need in this world and the world to come.

4
The Family Traits

Becoming a child of God is always marked by a change in lifestyle. Sometimes that change can be dramatic: the Philippian jailer bathed the wounds of the evangelists (*Acts 16:33*); the puzzled Ethiopian eunuch went on his way rejoicing (*Acts 8:39*); Zacchaeus repaid those he had cheated, fourfold (*Lk. 19:8*); Nicodemus eventually committed himself publicly to the cause of the gospel, a transformation perhaps less immediate, but no less real or profound (*Jn. 7:50–52; 19:38–42*).

Whenever a person is brought into the kingdom of God, and becomes a child of God, the new lifestyle follows. While God works in and through the personalities we already have (strictly speaking, we do not receive a 'new nature'), he begins to mark those personalities with certain broad similarities. There are characteristic qualities of life shared by all of God's children; there is a certain family likeness which is always present. We expect this in any family.

In our own families the children have many similar features, yet at the same time possess quite distinct and different personalities. It is the same in the family of God.

There are many obvious differences in God's children – 'sameness' is not something that appeals to God! Yet, at the same time, there are characteristics common to all members of the family, because they have received them from their Father in heaven, and learned them from their great Elder Brother.

This point is readily illustrated. From time to time I have had the privilege of meeting outstanding Christian leaders. What has often struck me forcefully is that despite differences in temperament, interests, and sometimes emphases, there are certain common features in their lives which would almost make you think that these individuals belong to the same family. But, of course, they do! That is why they exhibit the family likeness.

*   *   *

We have already noticed that we become God's children both by regeneration and by adoption. Those two dimensions influence us in different ways, just as our natural lives are influenced by both heredity and environment. Psychologists have long debated which plays the major role.

According to the New Testament our lifestyle is influenced both by the new life which has been given to us (we have been born of God) *and* by our adoption into the family of God. We receive new dispositions *and* enter a new environment. The wonderful thing about the gospel is that these two things are done together. Unlike a human adoption, God is able to give us the *disposition* of a member of his family. Yet, like natural adoption, we have come from another family, and God needs to keep on saying to us: 'Since you belong to *my* family now I want to see you behaving like one of *my* children!'

Generally speaking, it is the apostle John (in 1 John) who emphasises the relationship between the new birth and the new life, and it is the apostle Paul who emphasises the relationship between the new Fatherhood and the new lifestyle.

LIFE FROM A NEW BIRTH (THE TEACHING OF JOHN)

The purpose of the Gospel of John was to lead people to faith in Christ (*Jn. 20:31*). As a sequel, 1 John seems to have been written to clarify what it meant to be a Christian, and to assure those who were true Christians (*1 Jn. 5:13*). It contains what Robert Law (who wrote a commentary on the epistle under this title) called 'The Tests of Life'.

John expounds the characteristic marks of those who are children of God. He uses a variety of expressions for what it means to be a Christian: to know the Lord (*1 Jn. 2:3*); to be in the light (*2:9*); to know the truth (*2:20*), and so on. These were, in all likelihood, expressions current among the false teachers who were beginning to influence the early church. But the expression that John used most frequently to describe the true Christian was one who had been 'born of God' (see *1 Jn. 2:29; 3:9; 4:7; and 5:1, 4, 18*). John describes in some detail, therefore, *the effects of the new birth*.

John's teaching on the effects of the new birth can be summarised under four headings: a changed relationship to sin; a changed relationship to the church; a changed relationship to Christ; and a changed relationship to the world.

(1) *A changed relationship to sin*. John makes three startling statements during the course of his letter:

'No-one who lives in him [Christ] keeps on sinning' (*3:6*).

'No-one who is born of God will continue to
   sin' (*3:9*).
'We know that anyone born of God does not
   continue to sin' (*5:18*).

John's words are, if anything, even more stark than these
statements. The NIV translation is in part an *interpretation*
of what he is writing. It does not normally render the
present tense as a *present continuous*. Perhaps we should
understand John to be saying, quite simply: 'No one born
of God sins' (*not* 'keeps on sinning' as in NIV)!

Obviously John could not mean that the Christian is
never guilty of falling into sin, or that it is impossible truly
to be a Christian if we commit sin. That would be a
contradiction of his teaching earlier in the same letter: 'if
we claim to be without sin we deceive ourselves and the
truth is not in us' (*1:8*). Indeed, he emphasises the
reassuring fact that there is forgiveness for the Christian's
sins in Jesus Christ (*2:2*). Furthermore, as we look
forward to the day when we will be perfectly restored to
the image of Christ, we have a responsibility to *purify* our
lives (*3:3*). This would be unnecessary were we already
free from sin's influence.

What then did John mean? The simplest, and perhaps
the most obvious explanation is the one adopted in the
NIV translation. When we become Christians we do not
continue to sin the way we once did. We fail, but we do not
deliberately continue in a sinful lifestyle. We may not yet
be perfect, but we *are* different!

Alternatively, it has been suggested that John has some
definite sin in view. He may be saying: the Christian does
not continue in sin. There is a sin that is impossible for the
Christian to commit: to deny Christ irrevocably. 'There is
a sin which leads to death' (*5:16*). That sin appears to be
the denial of Christ (see *4:3*). Yet John's language ('does
not commit sin'; 'does not sin') seems too general for such

a *specific* act, particularly the specific act of rejecting Christ that is described elsewhere in the letter.

Perhaps the best way of understanding John's teaching here is by recognising that a new relationship with the world of sin and the dominion of darkness has been established in the life of the child of God. In both sections of John's letter where he describes the Christian as 'not sinning', he does so in the context of his adoption out of the family of the Evil One into the family of God. He is no longer under the dominion of the devil (in whose power John sees the whole world lying, *5:19*). Freed from those family ties, and from the legal reign of sin over his life, the Christian 'no longer sins'. Sin is no longer the characteristic feature of his lifestyle.

The question whether the Christian does actually commit sin is one John has already answered. For the moment he is concerned to emphasise that the Christian enjoys a radically new relationship to a power that once had altogether mastered his life.

If this is the correct way to understand John, his teaching has very definite parallels elsewhere in the New Testament.

Paul uses different thought structures to express the same basic doctrine. In Romans 5–6, he sees man as a slave in his relationship to Adam. Sin and Satan rule over his life. Indeed sin is the monarch of his being (*5:21; 6:17, 20*). Throughout these two chapters Paul seems to personify sin – he speaks of it as literally 'The Sin' (using the definite article). But through our rebirth in Jesus Christ, he argues, through our union with him by grace through faith, we have come to share in Christ's *death to sin* and *rebirth to God* (*6:5–11*). As brothers in the family of Christ, we have come to share in the characteristics of the Elder Brother.

Paul does not teach that we are sinless, any more than John does; but he does emphasise that in Christ we have been brought out of one kingdom into another. We have been born again into a new family, and the power of the Father of that family, the likeness of the Elder Brother in it, have been bestowed also on us. Yes, we sin and fail. But our lives grow in the settled direction of righteousness and holiness, because that is the nature of the family disposition given to us, and that is the direction in which our Elder Brother guides us.

John couples these two notions together beautifully in his letter. Why does the Christian 'not sin'? Because 'God's seed remains in him' (*1 Jn. 3:9*). As a child of God he shares in the holy nature of God through his fellowship with his glorified Saviour, Jesus Christ (compare *2 Pet. 1:4*). But as a brother in the family of God, he is also kept, protected, guided, and guarded by his Elder Brother – 'The one who was born of God keeps him safe, and the evil one does not touch him' (*1 Jn. 5:18*).

This is why John can turn his negative statements about our relationship to sin into positive ones: 'You know that everyone who *does what is right* has been born of him' (*2:29*). This is the hallmark of the family. Doing right is not the way *into* the kingdom; but it is the way of life in the kingdom. It is not the condition of regeneration, but its inevitable consequence and invariable accompaniment.

(2) *A changed relationship to the church.* John exhorts his readers to 'love one another' (*4:7*). He grounds this mutual Christian love in our common birth: 'Everyone who loves [i.e. in the sense just described] has been born of God and knows God.'

In this context, love means 'love for the Christian brothers'. The evidence that we belong to the family (and have been 'born of God') is our concern and affection for others who share in the new birth.

There is a constant emphasis on such family love throughout John's letter. Only those who love their brothers live in the light (*2:10*). It is because we love our brothers that we are assured that we have passed from death to life (*3:14*). Love is not a matter of words, but of reality – seeing a brother in need, taking pity on him, and extending practical help to him (*3:17–18*). In this way the love of God is brought to fruition or completion in us (*4:11–12*). To the apostle John this is obvious: 'Anyone who does not love his brother, whom he has seen, cannot love God, whom he has not seen' (*4:20*).

The new birth produces a moral transformation in our lives. As God's own children, we have a new relationship with one another, and a new attitude toward each other. The New Testament is full of this emphasis. It constantly declares that God does not create isolated individuals who have been born again by his Spirit. It is a *family* he is creating, in whom the mutual love of his own eternal family in the Trinity is reflected for the world to see (compare *Jn. 15:9; 17:20–23*).

The church is a family. Being members of the same family has far-reaching repercussions. Think of what it means to have a brother. You share with him the same parents, the same source of life. You have come from the union of the same flesh. There is a mysterious mutual participation, despite all your individual characteristics. In the same way, Christ became one flesh with us, as our Brother, and in him we become one with our fellow-believers (*Heb. 2:11, 14, 17*).

The implications of this family membership are far-reaching, in terms of our attitudes toward one another. *Not* to love our Christian brothers and sisters, *not* to seek their welfare, is an offence against the very nature of what it means to be a Christian. This is what John means when he says that it is utterly inconsistent to claim to love God, whom we have never seen, if we hate our brothers, whom we see daily.

(3) *A changed relationship to Christ.* One of the marks of

regeneration is always faith, or trust, in Christ: 'Everyone who believes that Jesus is the Christ is born of God' (*1 Jn. 5:1*).

These words have to be understood against a twofold background. First, there is the context of the false teaching that was confronting the church. Some teachers were debating and even denying the reality of the incarnation. John had already spoken about that in 1 John 4:1–3. Here he emphasises that right beliefs about Christ are vitally important.

Secondly, there is the background of the teaching on regeneration in John's Gospel, chapter 3. There, Jesus teaches Nicodemus that one of the effects of the new birth is faith in him as Saviour and Lord. The new birth is set in the context of faith in Christ as the way of salvation (*Jn. 3:16*).

How does new birth bring about faith? How does it have a noetic effect (an influence on our understanding and mental processes)? Regeneration is a birth God produces through the ministry of the word as well as by his Spirit (*Jas. 1:18, 1 Pet. 1:23*). It involves the opening of our spiritual eyes to understand the truth of the gospel, and the freeing of our wills to respond to it. In other words, *moral* transformation and *mental* transformation (believing in Jesus Christ) go together in regeneration.

Being a consistent child of God implies a particular understanding of and relationship to the Lord Jesus Christ.

(4) *A changed relationship to the world.* John's fourth mark of entrance into the family of God is that *we have overcome the world* (*1 Jn. 5:4*).

The word *world* is used with a tantalising variety of senses and nuances in Scripture. What John means here, in 1 John 5:4, is best determined by his use of 'world' elsewhere. In 1 John 5:19, he teaches that the whole world lies in the power of the Evil One. It is under the influence of the devil. Men, by nature, are in his kingdom rather than in the kingdom of God. But Christ has overcome the Evil One (he *came* to destroy the works of the devil – *1 Jn. 3:8*). He says to his people, 'Take heart! I have overcome the world' (*Jn. 16:33*). He has done so by his victory over Satan, and over all Satan's temptations. Through faith in Christ we also overcome the world.

John's language here is very unusual. 'Everyone who is born of God' is more accurately every *thing* born of God ('everyone' in the original text is neuter). Why should that be? Perhaps because the words for 'child' in Greek are neuter. It may also be because John is thinking of all Christians as belonging to a single category. He is not thinking about the experience of any specific Christian, but of what is true of everyone who is a Christian – true by definition, true by birth. Overcoming the world is part of his definition of what it means to be a Christian in the first place. Regeneration *means* victory, because regeneration takes place in Christ, the Victor who has already overcome the world.

John expands this idea of our victory in Christ. He says both that we *have overcome* in Christ, meaning the victory is already ours; and that we *are overcoming* (*1 Jn. 4:5*), meaning the battle *continues* to be engaged, and we *continue* to be involved in the fight.

This paradox of victory achieved yet continuing to be worked out is a fundamental pattern throughout the New Testament. We find it in Paul's teaching also. In Christ, he says, we have died to sin – it no longer rules over us. Yet we continue to battle against sin – we are not to let it reign over us (*Rom. 6:2, 12*). The decisive victory lies in the past, in the work of Jesus Christ, and has become ours through our fellowship with Christ. But we still continue to struggle against the defeated foe.

In practical terms, this struggle means that there are many things to which we will say 'no' as God's children, because they militate against our family ethos and loyalty to our 'Righteous Father' (*Jn. 17:25*). We are to put sin to death (*Rom. 8:13*). We are to take up the cross daily and follow Christ. Such crucifixion is not natural; it is a deliberate, brutal, painful putting to death. It is one means of execution that can never be carried out by the person being put to death. It symbolises to us that the world (in this sense) will not voluntarily lie down and die. It has to be dealt with radically by a consistent rejection of all that is evil in it.

Our victory is not easily gained, any more than was Christ's. To enter into the victory our Elder Brother gained means also entering into the struggle and strife of the Christian life. So, John says, 'This is the victory that has overcome the world, even our faith' (*1 Jn. 5:4*).

LIFE WITH A NEW FATHER (THE TEACHING OF PAUL)

The basic structure of John's thought is that we have been born again. The new life we have received works itself out in a variety of ways. The structure of much of the apostle Paul's thought is that since we have a new Father, and have been brought into a new family, we ought to live in a new way as his children.

Paul's teaching has sometimes been misunderstood. Indeed, much of the stress of earlier generations on the notion of the Fatherhood of God was intended to combat what was thought to be an overly Pauline emphasis in the understanding of the gospel. It was naively thought that Jesus taught the gospel of the Fatherhood of God, but Paul theologised it with his teaching on justification, introducing legal ways of thinking about salvation. On the contrary, however, Paul has a good deal to say about the

[49]

Fatherhood of God and the corresponding childhood of believers. We will explore other aspects of his teaching in later chapters; for now, we will focus on some fundamental elements in his teaching. In each case the movement of Paul's thought is: *since God is your Father, you should live a life that befits his children.*

What does this kind of life imply? For Paul, it meant basically two things. The first implication is, *we are to walk in the light.* As children of God, we become children of light (*1 Thess. 5:5*). Because we are in the light, we are to live as children of the light (*Eph. 5:8*). In the context of these statements Paul lays stress on two things: (1) we are no longer in the darkness, although we once were, and (2) we now belong to the light and to the day. Our identity is no longer what it used to be. We no longer belong to the old order of things, but to the new.

It would be utterly inconsistent and inappropriate, therefore, for us to adopt a lifestyle that was not characterised by moral light. It would be a denial of our birth, of God's Fatherhood, and of our family. Positively, we belong to the light. It is appropriate for us to live lives full of moral light. There are ethical expectations created by our standing in the family of Christ.

A second implication Paul draws for the life that befits God's children is, *we are to live as imitators of God.* In Ephesians 5:1, Paul makes the arresting statement: 'Be imitators of God' (the verb is the root of our word 'mimic'). Those words are grounded in what we are, through grace – 'as dearly loved children'. The consciousness of our God-given identity is intended to be an incentive for us to rise to the high calling of God in Christ Jesus, to imitate, mimic, copy, or model ourselves on the Father.

There is something completely appropriate about this exhortation. What could be more natural than a child imitating his father? But such a Father! Can we dare to imitate him? Paul is simply putting in a nutshell what Jesus had already taught the disciples: 'Be perfect, therefore, as your heavenly Father is perfect' (*Matt. 5:48*). Godlikeness, or godliness, is of the essence of the life of a child of God. When people observe our lives, they ought to be able to see the character of God in us, because as his children, we are those in whom his image has already begun to be restored.

This knowledge of our relationship to God is fundamental to Christian growth, and has a number of very practical implications.

First, it produces a sense of security. I am a child of God. He is my Father. He understands and cares for me. The Christian, of all people, should be increasingly aware of who he really is. That knowledge gives me stability in an unstable world. Knowing in the very depths of my being who I am, as I come increasingly to appreciate what it means to be a child of God, has a tremendously powerful effect. It sets me free from the world's anxious quest to 'be somebody'. (See Jesus' emphasis on this issue in Matthew 6:1–18. Freedom from the desire to be known as 'somebody' depends on knowing that 'your Father knows'.)

Secondly, this knowledge of our relationship to God produces a sense of direction. Belonging to God's family influences the general direction of my life, as well as giving me a new heart that expresses itself in a new lifestyle. In a rootless and directionless world I come from a family that has a purpose, shares the same standards, and aims at showing its Father's glory. To be a child of God is a blessing beyond calculation.

Thirdly, the knowledge that I am a child of God produces moral fibre. No longer do I need to be shaped and moulded by the world in which I live, and gear my life to the bondage of its reaction. I am a child in the family of God. His will and guidance, his instruction and discipline, are what I daily experience. In that context I learn to say 'no' to sin without being afraid of being negative! For I now see sin as utterly alien to the light and joy of the family in which I am being nurtured.

I am, of course, still liable to fall and sin. 'I have the desire to do what is good,' I often cry, 'but I cannot carry it out' (*Rom. 7:18*). The basic stance and direction of my whole life, however, is to be found in the context of my new family and my new Father. In his company, through his word, I know how to live. By the power of his Spirit I have the moral fibre woven into my being that helps me to live that way, for the praise of his glorious grace (*Eph. 1:5–6*).

5
Family Life

God sets the lonely in families, writes the psalmist (*Ps. 68:6*). That is true naturally. It is just as true spiritually. Just as children bear the image of their parents, so God creates his children in his image when he brings them into the family of his grace. He is, after all, the Father from whom the 'whole family in heaven and on earth derives its name' (*Eph. 3:15*). We are his children; we have his 'last name'. We belong to him and to each other as members of his family.

The moment we are born into the kingdom of God we become members of the family of God. We have new brothers and sisters. The Christian life brings not only a new Father and a new disposition, but also new family relationships. As children of God we cannot be solitary, isolationist, or individualistic. Just as we are to live in the light of our new Father's presence in our lives, and the new dispositions he has given to us, so we are also to live in the context of our family membership. Belonging to the household of faith (*Gal. 6:10, Eph. 2:19*) involves many new privileges and requires that we recognise certain new responsibilities.

This idea, that we are not only Christians, but as such are brothers (which in the language of the New Testament *includes* 'sisters'!) profoundly influences the way we are to think and live. 'Brother' is one of the most emotive words in the human vocabulary. In the language of the New Testament the word is *adelphos*. It is a compound word (*a* = 'from' and *delphus* = 'womb') and conveys the idea of coming from the same womb. This is what makes brothers special. They come from the same parents; at one time they inhabited the same dark, mysterious world of their mother's womb. They share a common origin, and from the beginning have shared a common environment. No other relationship in life has those features.

According to the New Testament, the same is true of Christians. We have been given 'new birth into a living hope through the resurrection of Jesus Christ from the dead' (*1 Pet. 1:3*). The 'womb' which has given us new life is the empty tomb of Jesus. Through the power of his resurrection we have been given new birth and share in a common inheritance which can never perish, spoil, or fade (*1 Pet. 1:4*).

Our common family tie explains the wonderful phenomenon that every Christian experiences whenever he moves from one area of his country to another, or from one continent to another: those who belong to the family of God share a common family likeness and recognise one another. Language, culture and education may all be different, but a common bond – we might even say common genetic structure created by the Spirit – unites us as members of the same family. We have the same Father, the same Elder Brother, the same family code, the same inheritance. No wonder we learn quickly to appreciate each other!

That is not to say that members of the family never quarrel with each other, or that there is never any need for family correction and discipline, or that there are no 'black sheep'. But all of that has to be seen in the family context (for failure to do so has been the cause of much sorrow and unhappiness throughout church history).

THE FAMILY RULE

In a properly ordered family, the father's word is the rule – or should be. It expresses his knowledge, experience, and wisdom. His children may not always understand *why* he says certain things or plans certain courses of action. Sometimes he may explain his reasons and purposes; at other times he knows his children will be happiest *not knowing* (although they assume they will always be happier if they know!).

This discretion need not be a stumbling-block in a healthy family with a healthy father. Such a father demonstrates from the beginning of the family's life that his character and his word can be trusted implicitly, even when he does not explain his actions.

Nothing is worse for a family than to have a father whose word cannot be trusted. Correspondingly, at the heart of all truly joyful family life is a father (or parent) whose word is his bond. To such a father, the children can say: 'But you promised', and receive the answer, 'Indeed, I did; and therefore it shall be!'

This is how life is to be lived in the family of God. *The Father's word is rule.* The word is enshrined for us in the pages of Scriptures. When we say, as we read God's word, 'I have hidden your word in my heart that I might not sin against you' (*Ps. 119:11*), we are reflecting our family upbringing. We are recognising that our Father's word has slowly become part of us, and has so influenced the way we think that we have no desire to do anything (sin against him) which would grieve or in any way offend him.

[55]

As God's children, we need to learn to read and hear Scripture in this frame of mind. It is the 'word of encouragement that *addresses you as sons*' (*Heb. 12:5*). We should come to it as those who are listening to their Father – which is, after all, precisely what we are doing!

This attitude toward Scripture has an important bearing, too, on the place of God's word in our more public gatherings. Since the time of the Reformation (which was characterised by a recovery of the sense of the Fatherhood of God), the gatherings of God's children have been marked by special attention to his word. Consequently, preaching or biblical exposition has occupied a central place in worship. That emphasis has declined in two ways.

Where the gospel has ceased to be believed, less and less emphasis has been placed on God's word – inevitably so. That is why in recent times many theological schools and faculties have required less study of the biblical languages and more study of human psychology or sociology. These things are important, but they do not determine the meaning of what God says in his word. Inevitably, where his word is no longer believed, its real meaning is no longer of primary importance for the church. The decline of preaching in churches permeated by liberalism is exactly what we would expect.

Attention to God's word has also declined where *celebration* has taken the place of *listening*. In recent years there has been a widespread recovery of the biblical truth that the Lord is great and greatly to be praised. We are to celebrate him. How we need to learn to do that! But often this emphasis has gone hand-in-hand with relegating the exposition of the whole of God's word for all of God's people. It cannot ever be right to celebrate God's works at the expense of listening to God's word. In fact, the child who never properly listens to everything his father says tends to become obnoxious! He develops an independent spirit that manifests itself frequently when any attempt is made to subdue him. Just at that point he is likely to turn round and point out the faults of his other brothers and sisters, instead of taking the rebuke that his father is administering to *him*.

Paul outlines the proper place for the Father's word in his final instructions and encouragement to Timothy. Paul uses terminology reminiscent of the counsel of the father to his son in the early chapters of Proverbs. He reminds Timothy that the Scriptures are able to make him 'wise for salvation through faith in Christ Jesus' (*2 Tim. 3:15*). He continues to use the language of a father–son relationship when he describes the 'useful' nature of God's word for 'teaching, rebuking, correcting and training in righteousness' (*2 Tim. 3:16*).

This language describes exactly the function of a father's education of his children. Fathers *teach* their children. Their instruction provides a frame of reference and guidance for the whole of life. Moreover, fathers sometimes need to *rebuke* their children, when their lives do not conform to the teaching they have received. A father must learn to say 'no' to his children, or they will grow up without either discernment or inner discipline.

Fathers must also *correct* their children. In this context, 'correct' carries a restorative connotation. Paul's word is used outside of the New Testament for the setting and healing of a broken limb. It is used in the New Testament itself only here, but it clearly carries the same positive overtones. A father's correction is health-giving. Finally, fathers *train* their children in the right ways, in order that they may grow into mature men and women who have the equipment for life (*2 Tim. 3:17*). Unless parents have this long-term view, they become slaves to the immediate and, foolishly, perhaps even slaves to their children!

All this fatherly education is supremely true of the influence of the word of God the Father Almighty. As his children we should allow ourselves to be exposed to it constantly, and to become so familiar with it that its contents become virtually second nature to us.

Incidentally, notice in this context that there is no ultimate conflict between law and love in the family of God. Both are expressions of the Father's purpose for our lives. Indeed, his law springs from his love. It is only when the child is at odds with the Father that his rule will seem restrictive or harsh.

THE FAMILY FELLOWSHIP

The Father rules his family through his word. But in that word he supplies a rule that governs our relations: *Love one another*.

This rule is exemplified and taught by our Elder Brother, Jesus Christ. Just as he has loved us, so we are to love one another (*Jn. 15:12, 17*). Paul similarly describes the rules governing the fellowship of the church ('clothe yourselves with compassion, kindness, humility, gentleness and patience. Bear with each other and forgive whatever grievances you may have against one another. Forgive as the Lord forgave you'). He adds: 'And over all these virtues put on love, which binds them all together in perfect unity' (*Col. 3:12–14*). Love is the common element in the family characteristics. Without it the family lifestyle will be formal and ultimately hypocritical.

John Owen, the great seventeenth-century English theologian, expresses this point vividly. He says that the family of God is like a man going into the forest to gather wood for his fire. He collects the branches he sees lying around him. But as he does so he realises he has a problem. How is he going to get them home? One branch is thick, another thin; one is long, another short; one is straight, another crooked. So he binds them together with a cord, and in this way he is able to carry them home in one bundle. This, says Owen, is the way Christ works in his church. How can such different people possibly live together as one family? Only if they are bound together by the cord of love. Only as we realise that we have a common Father, a shared birth, the same Elder Brother, the same family characteristics, and *therefore* love one another, can our fellowship be what the Lord wants to make it.

This emphasis on loving each other has several important practical implications.

We are to learn to accept and appreciate one another, no matter what natural differences might separate us. In the New Testament it is James who does most of the straight talking on this theme: rich and poor alike are to be treated as brothers. There is to be no favouritism: 'Listen, *my dear brothers*: Has not God chosen those who are poor in the eyes of the world to be rich in faith and to inherit the kingdom he promised those who love him?' James implies that failure to treat our brothers as brothers is to *insult* them (*Jas. 2:5–6*).

James goes even further. To speak against a brother is to speak *against the law* (*Jas. 4:11*). Doubtless James has in mind Jesus' exposition of the law: in the Sermon on the Mount, slander is simply another form of murder. It may not kill the body, but it assassinates another's personality and his rightful reputation before men (*Matt. 5:21–22*).

But there is a further development of our family fellowship. Our acceptance of each other is to be much more than a grudging and reluctant handshake! We are positively to welcome one another, and to learn to appreciate one another's gifts and contributions to the family life we enjoy together. There is to be no sibling rivalry in God's family!

This harmony requires a genuine embracing of one another – even when there are matters of personal practice on which we disagree. Christ has accepted and welcomed us *in order to bring praise to God* (*Rom. 15:7*). We should follow his example because he is our Elder Brother, and also because to do so *shows* the character of the Father who has accepted and welcomed us in Christ, even when we were sinners (*2 Cor. 5:19*).

In particular Paul directs our brotherly appreciation toward those in the family who enjoy less prestige. We are a body in which 'those parts . . . that seem to be weaker are indispensable, and the parts that we think are less honourable we treat with special honour. And the parts that are unpresentable are treated with special modesty, while our presentable parts need no special treatment. But God has combined the members of the body and has given greater honour to the parts that lacked it, *so that there should be no division in the body*, but that its parts should have equal concern for each other' (*1 Cor. 12:22–25*).

Have you ever seen a well-adjusted family cope with a brother or sister who is physically or mentally retarded? It is deeply moving to watch the mixture of special discipline and grace that makes such a family member not only belong, but actually be treated as special in the family circle. So it should be in the family of God. He has commanded it in the word by which he directs and disciplines his family – yes, and rebukes and corrects them too!

Alas, we show all too little of this – and so the world sees all too little of our light shining before men 'that they may see your good deeds and praise *your Father* in heaven' (*Matt. 5:16*).

In addition to accepting or welcoming one another, in the family of God we are to learn to forgive, and, where necessary, restore one another. If we have grievances against one another, these are to be forgiven, just as the Lord has forgiven us (*Col. 3:13*). If one of our brothers is caught in sin, we are to restore him gently (*Gal. 6:1*). He is our *brother*. That is what Paul sees as the determining factor in our reaction to him.

This loving restoration needs to be placed in the wider New Testament context in order to underline the discipline and grace in the mutual care of the family life of the church. An illustration appears in the church family in Thessalonica. Despite Paul's teaching, some of the brethren had become idle. Paul warns the rest of the family to 'keep away from *every brother* who is idle and does not live according to the teaching you received from us' (*2 Thess. 3:6*). But at the same time, Paul exhorts them – while they are to seek to help such brothers feel ashamed – to treat them *as brothers*, not as enemies (*2 Thess. 3:14–15*).

Such a mixture of discipline and forgiveness is conceivable only within a family context. It is developed even further in the case of the grievous sin that took place in the church family at Corinth. When it was eventually dealt with, Paul urged the church to comfort the penitent so that he would not be overwhelmed with a sense of guilt. They should reaffirm their love for him and assure him that he was forgiven, lest Satan (the family enemy, and particularly the enemy of the Father and Elder Brother) cause division within the household of faith (*2 Cor. 2:7–11*).

No family finds failure easy to handle. The church is no exception. The Father's reputation is at stake. But the Father has already abandoned his reputation by giving his Son for our salvation! The real problem is so often *our* reputation. We cope badly with the failure of a brother. Why? Because we place the estimation of outsiders to the family above the concerns of the family and its members. This should not be. The family is at fault when it does not deal with its failures.

CHILDREN OF THE LIVING GOD

Only when we realise that the church is a family, that we are brothers and sisters in that family, will we have a right perspective from which to view those who fail badly, and a right motive to see them disciplined faithfully, and welcomed back with many reaffirmations of our love.

We do not always realise the extent to which such family love requires the self-discipline and even self-denial of family members. But that is implicit in the loss of reputation which may be involved in mutual acceptance, particularly in welcoming back into the family those who have wandered from it but are now restored. It was this *self-denial* that Jesus noted was lacking in the lives of so many of the Pharisees. They could not tolerate the attitude that welcomed prodigal sons back to the Father. It would have required a loss of face on their part to join in the Father's celebration (*Lk. 15:28–30*). But such self-forgetfulness is required of all those who belong to God's family.

In a rather different context Paul stresses the need for self-denial. There are some matters over which Christians are divided. Some Christians have scruples about certain activities. In Paul's day that included what a Christian could eat and drink (because meat offered for sale in the market-place had often previously been part of a pagan religious ritual). Paul's principle here was straightforward and categorical: 'If what I eat causes *my brother* to fall into sin, I will never eat meat again, so that I will not cause him to fall' (*1 Cor. 8:13*). In his view, the very existence of his family relationship as a brother demanded a simple and radical attitude. Loving his brother might mean saying 'no' to something that Paul himself regarded as altogether legitimate. It would be well for us, and for the whole family of God, if we followed his example. But we should be forewarned: it will be like going on a diet – painful until our desires have been mastered and we have learned to

deny ourselves for the sake of higher and greater consider-
ations.

These, then, are all part of what it means to 'keep on
loving each other as brothers' (*Heb. 13:1*).

THE FAMILY EMBLEMS

In our home we have a plaque hanging on the wall. It is a
shield covered with our family tartan on which are
mounted the family emblem and the family motto. My
family motto is *Dulcius ex asperis*. It reflects on how
sweeter things may come from the *bitter* experiences of
life. The emblem itself shows a bee sucking nectar from a
thorny Scots thistle! The words explain the meaning of the
picture; the picture illustrates and conveys what is meant
by the motto.

Many families have such emblems, and the family of
God is no exception. Its emblems are baptism and the
Lord's Supper. Both point, of course, to the work of the
Elder Brother: to the privilege of being united to him, in
the case of baptism; and to the continuing privilege of
enjoying communion with him, in the case of the Lord's
Supper. But they also remind us of what is involved in
belonging to the family of God.

Baptism underlines that we have all been brought into
the body of Christ by one and the same Spirit (*1 Cor.
12:13*). Likewise, we break one loaf and drink from one
cup in the Lord's Supper (*1 Cor. 10:16–17*). Thus, we who
are many individuals show ourselves to be one in Jesus
Christ. That is why one effect of using these emblems will
always be the breakdown of those divisions and barriers
separating one individual from another.

The celebration of the Lord's Supper carries with it
a special significance. For the family of God, it is like
the wedding rehearsal meal so common among North

American families. We celebrate, but only in anticipation of the wedding day; as a family we give thanks for the past, but with a view to what will soon take place. It is in this spirit that we come to the Lord's table, and remember Christ's death 'until he comes' (*1 Cor. 11:26*). Today, the family celebrates the Lord's Supper; soon we will celebrate the Marriage Supper of the Lamb. Each Lord's Supper is a family anticipation of that great day, and reminds us also of the final reunion of all the members of the family in the presence of the Father and the Elder Brother.

ACCESS TO THE FATHER

One further privilege is a feature of the life of the family of God. It is one of the marks of a true father that, no matter who he may be, how busy or important, his children have a unique privilege of access to him. He may be a king, or a powerful businessman, or a scientific genius, but his children call him 'father'. More than anything else, perhaps, this is the distinguishing mark of genuine Christian faith; we are given the privilege of calling God 'Father'. We enter into his presence in the consciousness that we belong, and are at home with him.

This is what prayer really means: knowing that we have a secure relationship with God in which we can address him in the knowledge that he cares, and has the power to aid us.

A friend of mine adopted a child into his family when he was in another country. He tells of the days that passed after she was adopted in which he knew that the father–daughter relationship he longed to enjoy with her had not yet bonded. Then one day she appeared at the side of his desk with one of her shoes in her hand: 'Daddy,' she said, 'I need another shoelace.' That was the first time she had ever called him by that name. She dared to approach him, despite all her initial reservations, and in her little need call him 'father'. This is what happens when we understand what it means to be adopted into God's family and be born anew by his Spirit. We have confidence to speak with him about our needs and to ask for his help.

Addressing God as 'Father' in prayer seems to have been unknown in the Jewish religion in Palestine before the ministry of Jesus. In a general way, of course, there was the recognition that God was the Father of the nation (for example, *Is. 63:16; 64:8*). But what was unique in Jesus' address to God was the way in which he called him *'Abba*, Father'. Joachim Jeremias writes that while *'we do not have a single example* of God being addressed as "Abba" in Judaism . . . Jesus *always* addressed God in this way in his prayers'.[1]

In fact, that is not strictly accurate. There was *one* occasion on which the Elder Brother addressed God without calling him Father – on the cross, when he cried out, 'My God, my God, why have you forsaken me?' The moment in Jesus' life that, above all other moments, gained us access into the presence of God as 'Abba, Father', is that moment when Jesus apparently ceased to be conscious of that Fatherly presence and love. This underlines the cost of our adoption: the Elder Brother had to enter into the desolation and isolation of the cross and experience the loneliness and alienation due all his brothers as he bore their sin. That is why Paul says it is through *the blood of Christ* that we have *access to the Father* (*Eph. 2:18*). We should never forget the cost to God of the privilege of prayer we enjoy. Recognising and appreciating it enables us to maintain the spirit of reverence and filial familiarity which we see in Jesus' own life of prayer.

The knowledge that God is the Father of his children

[1]Joachim Jeremias, *New Testament Theology*, trans. J. Bowden (London: S.C.M. Press, 1971), p. 66.

dominates Jesus' teaching on prayer, and explains the spirit in which he encourages us to pray.

Jesus encourages us to pray *simply*. This distinguishes the child of God from the hypocrite. The hypocrite is so unsure of his relationship to God (and rightly so!) that he thinks of prayer in terms of its length and eloquence; the child of God knows he is speaking to his Father, and talks simply and directly. The hypocrite foolishly thinks that God is impressed by the same things that impress his fellow-men. He does not understand what it means for God to be the Father who knows only too well what is really in men's hearts.

When Jesus teaches his disciples to pray – in the petitions in the Lord's Prayer, for example – he shows them simple directness. Since 'your Father knows what you need before you ask him' (*Matt. 6:8*), and *we know he knows*, we can speak freely, straightforwardly, definitely.

Jesus also encourages us to pray *boldly*. In the parable of the friend who disturbed his neighbour at midnight, Jesus tells us how the petitioner received what he wanted – not because he was a friend, but 'because of the man's persistence'. The word 'persistence' is really 'shameless-ness' (*anaideia, Lk. 11:8*). It is the sheer effrontery of the man, his transgressing of the bounds of propriety, that Jesus seems to commend.

Such boldness – which would be sheer impudence in a neighbour – is the privilege of the children in the family. It can be abused – and sometimes in the pride and egocentricity of some of our lives it is – as though the Father were to come at our beck and call. Yet in faithful children, this bold asking is really based on the Father's promise to do for us whatever we ask in Jesus' name. Just as the neighbour knew that his friend had bread to meet his need, so the Father has promised us that he is able to meet all our needs. It is on the basis of the Father's riches and on the strength of his promise that we can speak to him with such directness.

This confidence is the explanation for the prayer life of Elijah. James says he was no different from us (*Jas. 5:17–18*). But he possessed the promise God had given that if his people turned from him, he would shut up the heavens against them (*Deut. 28:15–24*). All Elijah was doing was asking God to keep his promise, and expressing his confidence that he would! This is the high privilege of every child of God.

Jesus also teaches us to pray *expectantly*. In his teaching, our Lord was, apparently, fond of using a particular kind of logical reasoning known as an argument *a minore ad maius* (from the lesser to the greater). In such an argument it is reasoned that if the lesser position (or easier, or more obvious) be true, then the greater position must be all the more true. In connection with the Fatherhood of God, he used the following argument: 'If you, then, though you are evil, know how to give good gifts to your children, *how much more* will your Father in heaven give good gifts to those who ask him!' (*Matt. 7:11*). The argument is: You are evil, yet you love your children and give them gifts; God is good, and loves his children perfectly. You may be confident, then, that he will shower gifts on his children.

That does not mean that we will get what we ask for in the precise way we expect it. God may answer our prayers by 'crosses', as the hymn-writer John Newton put it. But it is inconceivable that the Father should fail to give good things to his children. That is why, having prayed, we can live in the expectation that, one day, in some way, those prayers will be answered. For the child of God then, the whole of life becomes an answered prayer. And prayer becomes simply the living of the whole of our lives in the light of the Father's promise and in the presence of the Father's love.

To live in the light of God's promises and love, we need to be assured of our filial relation to him. This confidence is what the Spirit of sonship brings to us, as we will see in the next chapter.

6
The Spirit of Adoption

So far we have seen that God works at several levels in our lives. He brings us into his family by giving us new birth; new dispositions are created in us because we belong to a new creation. He also gives us the rights and privileges of sons through adoption. We have a new name. We become heirs of all that Christ has done for us; indeed, we come to share in Christ's own inheritance as joint-heirs with him (*Rom. 8:17*).

God works also on another plane. We saw earlier how the parable of the prodigal son epitomises the disposition of some Christians, even when they are restored to fellowship with God. Lurking in their hearts there often remains this sneaking suspicion: 'I am not worthy to be God's son, but perhaps I can struggle through as one of his hired servants.'

At the root of such thinking is an inability to believe that salvation is entirely of God's grace and love. We contribute nothing to it; we can do nothing to earn it in any way. We are often slow to realise the implications of that. We are sons, but we are in danger of having the mindset of hired servants. Furthermore, if there is nothing else the devil can do to mar our joy in Christ, he will try to produce in us what our forefathers used to call a 'bondage frame of spirit'.

We can detect traces of this bondage developing in the opening pages of the Bible, when the serpent came to Eve and said: 'Did God really say, "You must not eat from any tree in the garden"?' (*Gen. 3:1*). His aim was to suggest to Adam and Eve: 'Do you really understand the kind of God who has set you here? He doesn't really want the best for you because he is restricting you. He has made you his hired servants to look after this garden, but he will not allow you to enjoy it.'

As a matter of fact, they were free to enjoy every tree in the garden except one (*Gen. 2:16–17*). That was the very reverse of the serpent's suggestion. God had set them in the garden as his children! It was theirs. But they fell for Satan's trick, and were deceived into thinking they were hired servants and not children. Tragically, they became what they wrongly thought themselves to be. Precisely the same kind of temptation faces us as children of God. That is why we need the Spirit of adoption.

What is this Spirit of adoption? Paul says: 'You did not receive a spirit that makes you a slave again to fear, but you received the Spirit of sonship. And by him we cry, "*Abba*, Father." The Spirit himself testifies with our spirit that we are God's children. Now if we are children, then we are heirs – heirs of God and co-heirs with Christ, if indeed we share in his sufferings in order that we may also share in his glory' (*Rom. 8:15–17*).

Many modern translations render the Greek word *huiothesia* in this passage as 'sonship'. That tends to obscure what Paul says. The word Paul uses means, literally, being placed as a son. It is the word for adoption, or perhaps better, sonship by adoption. Paul is, therefore, thinking about the Spirit of sonship in relation to the idea of our *adoption* rather than our *regeneration*.

What, or who, is the Spirit of adoption or sonship? Is the reference to our (human) spirit, or to the (divine) Spirit? The context suggests that Paul is referring to the Holy Spirit. He makes constant reference to him in the previous verses (*Rom. 8:2, 4, 5, 6, 9, 11, 13, 14, 16!*). Furthermore, the parallel passage in Galatians 4:1–6 speaks of this Spirit as the Spirit of the Son (*4:6*). What is in view, then, in the Spirit of sonship, is the presence in our life of the One who was present in the life and ministry of *the* Son of God, supporting him, assuring him, enabling him, too, to cry, '*Abba*, Father' (*Mk. 14:36*, cf. Rom. 8:15).

The ministry of the Spirit of adoption brings us to a deep-seated persuasion that we really are the sons of God. If it is a fact that we have new dispositions, that God has adopted us into his family, then the Spirit assures us this is true, and enables us to live in the enjoyment of such a rich spiritual blessing.

Paul underlines the significance of the Spirit's work by means of a contrast. We have received the Spirit of adoption, *not the spirit of bondage*. It is difficult to know whether Paul is speaking here of our spirit or the Holy Spirit, but in either case the effect is the same – bondage to fear.

What is the point of this contrast? We should use the parallel passage in Galatians 4:1–6 to help us interpret Paul's meaning. There he is contrasting the experience of God's grace in Christ with the comparative 'bondage' that believers knew under the old covenant. They were sons then, but the time set by God for the full inheritance of his grace had not yet come. By comparison (and *only* by comparison, since believers in the old covenant experienced large measures of joy), those were days of bondage.

[71]

But now believers are inheritors of all the rich experience of free-born sons. To bring that to fruition, God sent his Son to secure salvation and forgiveness. Then he sent his Spirit into our hearts to create childlike, filial dispositions there, to bring us into the full enjoyment and experience of his saving grace.

Yet there is another, more personal aspect to this contrast. Paul emphasises that formerly we lived in fear, but now we live as sons, at liberty. Before we became Christians, we had no security – we were under Satan's power and subject to the fear of death. Because we were subject to the greatest of fears, we were in bondage to all manner of lesser fears (*Heb. 2:15*). Now God has released us from that condition. Christ has removed our guilt. Furthermore, he sends his Spirit into our hearts, bringing us the deep spiritual and psychological security that rests on the objective fact that our sins are forgiven and we belong to the Lord. This is the spirit that is taught in the great catechism published by Zacharias Ursinus and Casper Olevianus in 1563, known as *The Heidelberg Catechism*, and used by many European churches as a confession of faith. The first question and answer are:

Question 1. What is your only comfort in life and in death?

Answer. That I, with body and soul, both in life and in death, am not my own, but belong to my faithful Saviour Jesus Christ, who with his precious blood has fully satisfied for all my sins, and redeemed me from all the power of the devil; and so preserves me that without the will of my Father in heaven not a hair can fall from my head: indeed all things must minister to my salvation. Therefore, by his Holy Spirit he also assures me of everlasting life, and makes me willing and ready in heart henceforth to live unto him.

We have, indeed, the Spirit of adoption, and, consequently, the Spirit of sons and daughters of our Father!

The Spirit of adoption produces a series of important effects on the Christian.

First, *the Spirit of adoption gives us assurance*. The Spirit, in his ministry as the Spirit of adoption, bears witness with our spirit (probably not 'to our spirit') that we are the children of God (*Rom. 8:16*).

What is this 'witness'? These words have been the subject of much discussion by Christians over many centuries. There are two mistakes which we can make in thinking about them. One mistake is thinking of this testimony of the Spirit in exclusively mystical terms, as though the Spirit whispered to us in some ineffable experience, 'You are a child of God.' That would amount to a new revelation from God *over and above* the revelation given to us in Scripture. The other mistake is to reduce the supernatural element in what Paul says. Sometimes we can be so afraid of a wrong emphasis on mystical experience that we actually deny the supernatural work of God in our lives. It may well be that this Spirit-given assurance will be experienced in wonderful, even dramatic, ways.

It is best for us to build up Paul's teaching in stages. To begin, we should notice that in Paul's teaching the Spirit's witness is a *joint* witness, a witness '*with* our spirit' (*Rom. 8:16*), and not an *independent* witness. It is *with* the witness of our own spirit that the Holy Spirit bears his witness – that we are children of God.

The background to this may lie in the teaching of Deuteronomy 19:15: 'A matter must be established by the testimony of two or three witnesses.' The Spirit is the witness who gives credibility to the witness of our own spirit.

We might think, for example, of the context of the Roman practice of adoption, which is the background of Paul's teaching in Romans 8. Adoption was a public act. It was performed before witnesses. Those witnesses were, at a later date, able to give testimony to the fact of someone's adoption. In a dispute (over an inheritance, for example) the person's own testimony was coupled with that of the witnesses. In the same sense, the Spirit of God confirms our self-awareness through his testimony.

Why should this be so important? The Christian is often the object of satanic attack and is tempted to doubt his real standing before God. Paul alludes to this later in Romans 8, when he faces a series of questions that had obviously exercised his mind and heart at various times: *Who* can be against us? *Who* will bring any charge against those whom God has chosen? *Who* is he that condemns? *Who* shall separate us from the love of Christ? (*Rom. 8:31–35*). The one who tries to do these things is Satan. We therefore stand in need of a 'friend in court' who will take our side and say: 'This is a child of God.' That is exactly what the Spirit of God does.

John Owen, in his famous work on *Communion with God*, expressed this when he wrote about the witness of the Spirit:

> An allusion it is to judicial proceedings in point of titles and evidences. The judge being set, the person concerned lays his claim, produceth his evidences, and pleads them; his adversaries endeavouring all that in them lies to invalidate them, and disannul his plea, and to cast him in his claim. In the midst of the trial, a person of known and approved integrity comes into the court, and gives testimony fully and directly on the behalf of the claimer; which stops the mouths of all his adversaries, and fills the man that pleaded with joy and satisfaction. So is it in this case. The soul, by the power of its own conscience, is brought before the law of God. There a man puts in his plea – that he is a child of God, that he belongs to God's family; and for this end produceth all his evidences, every thing whereby faith

gives him an interest in God. Satan, in the meantime, opposeth with all his might; sin and law assist him; many flaws are found in his evidences; the truth of them all is questioned; and the soul hangs in suspense as to the issue. In the midst of the plea and contest the Comforter comes, and, by a word of promise or otherwise, overpowers the heart with a comfortable persuasion (and bears down all objections) that his plea is good, and that he is a child of God.

When our spirits are pleading their right and title, he comes in and bears witness on our side; at the same time enabling us to put forth acts of filial obedience, kind and child-like; which is called 'crying, *Abba*, Father' (*Gal. 4:6*).[1]

Next, we should notice that the witness of the Spirit is related to the cry that issues from our hearts: '*Abba*, Father.' It is 'by him' (the Spirit) that we utter this cry. Is this cry itself the witness of the Spirit with our spirits? Or is this cry the result of that witness? The witness of the Spirit is expressed in the actual act of crying out '*Abba*, Father', as Jesus did in the Garden of Gethsemane (*Mk. 14:36*). In this very cry for help, the Spirit of God bears witness *with our spirits* that we are indeed God's children. He works in the inner recesses of our being to persuade us that we belong to the Father. It is that deep, inward consciousness that comes to the surface in times of crisis, when we still call God '*Abba*, Father'.

This interpretation is confirmed by the fact that in Galatians 4:6, Paul says that it is the Holy Spirit (*not* our spirit) who cries out '*Abba*, Father.' Taking these two passages together, we conclude that it is *by the Spirit* that *we* are enabled to cry out, '*Abba*, Father.' In this, our spirit bears its witness and the Holy Spirit confirms the

[1]John Owen, op. cit., p. 241.

testimony of our own spirit, that we are in fact the children of God.

It is interesting to notice that Paul speaks of believers as having 'the firstfruits of the Spirit' (*Rom. 8:23*). He does not mean that we have only part (the first part) of the Spirit, but that the Spirit himself is the firstfruits of our inheritance. The word he uses (*aparchē*) was also used to describe the birth certificate of a free man! Perhaps this nuance was present in Paul's mind here, too, in a passage that is dealing so much with the concept of the believer as a son of God, adopted into his family. So, the Spirit serves as our 'birth certificate', actively engaging in our lives to assure us that we belong to the Father!

Paul's teaching here helps us to answer a thorny question: Do we have assurance because we have certain marks of true faith, *or* because we have the witness of the Spirit? The question is really a false antithesis. Paul's emphasis on the Spirit's witness does not negate the consciousness the believer already has as he trusts in Christ and sees the fruit of that trust emerge in his life. The two go hand in hand. In fact, the harmony between the witness of the Spirit and the fruit of the Spirit is underlined by Paul in his treatment of the other aspects of the ministry of the Spirit of adoption.

The second effect of the Spirit of adoption on the believer is the mortification of sin. Paul makes it plain that the Spirit has an *ethical* influence on the life of the Christian. He is the *Holy* Spirit.

Throughout Romans 8 Paul underlines the nature of the Spirit's ministry. In verse 15 he identifies him as the Spirit of sonship. Notice the reasoning leading to that description:

The way of life is the way of putting to death the misdeeds of the body, through the Spirit (*verse 13*).

Next, ethical reformation characterises those who are

'led by the Spirit' (*verse 14*). They are the sons of God.

The Spirit we received is the Spirit of sonship. We can expect him to work in us in the way just described (*verse 15*).

The logic of Paul's reasoning is that if we are sons and have received the Spirit of sonship, it follows that our lives should be marked by a 'putting to death the misdeeds of the body'. That will be accomplished in the power of the Spirit, who is the Spirit of adoption. Expressed succinctly, the Spirit of adoption is also the Spirit of mortification.

How, then, do we mortify the misdeeds of the body in the power of the Spirit? We need to do so out of right motives, and in a right manner.

In our motives, we have an obligation to mortify sin. Paul says, 'Therefore, brothers, we have an obligation – but it is not to the sinful nature [the flesh], to live according to it' (*Rom. 8:12*). The implication is that we have an obligation to live according to the Spirit. Where do we get this obligation? It springs from the fact that we are 'controlled by the Spirit' (*Rom. 8:9*). We are under his Lordship and direction – Paul actually says we are 'in the Spirit'. The Spirit is the sphere in which we conduct our lives; he is the principle by which we live them. In that sphere, the Spirit seeks to establish a lifestyle that is contrary to the direction of the flesh. He produces a conflict with the flesh. The aim of that conflict is to minimise the influences and tendencies of the flesh, to destroy its works and plant the fruit of the Spirit (*Gal. 5:17–26*).

Further, the Spirit who thus rules us is the Spirit of the resurrection. He is 'the Spirit of him who raised Jesus from the dead' and Paul adds that he is 'living in you' (*Rom 8:11*). He is the Spirit of the new age that dawned first in the experience of Jesus Christ. Although we do not yet experience the powers of that new age fully, we do partially because the Spirit is in our lives. He belong to that new age, and all his work in us is to urge us to live lives here and now that are appropriate to our future destiny.

Paul suggests that we have another motive to put to death indwelling sin; this is how children should live – seeking to please their Father in all things, shunning everything that might displease him in any way. Those who are thus led by the Spirit are God's sons (*Rom. 8:14*). These words, often taken to refer to God's guidance, really underline the holy behaviour of God's children. The leading of the Spirit is not so much guidance about particular steps in our lives, but guidance about the moral direction we are always to take.

A final motivation concerns the consequences of living according to the flesh: 'If you live according to the flesh, you will die' (*Rom. 8:13*, RSV). Why this brutal frankness? The fact that Paul's words here are reminiscent of God's words to Adam and Eve (*Gen. 2:17*) provides the answer. They were led astray, taking the word of God with less than the seriousness it merited. They fell to the serpent's temptation that involved a denial of God's word (*Gen. 3:4*). 'Do not think that you are immune to a similar failure,' Paul is saying. 'Take sin seriously!' Do not be hardened by the deceitfulness of sin (*Heb. 3:13*).

How, then, do we put to death the misdeeds of the body? First of all, we should live our lives under the all-seeing eye of our Father and in the knowledge that we will appear before his judgement seat. This is not only expressed by Paul (*2 Cor. 5:10*); it is at the heart of Jesus' teaching on the Christian life in the Sermon on the Mount. Our Father sees and knows; our Father responds by way of judgement. It will be no security on the Last Day for us to say, 'Lord, Lord, did we not prophesy in your name, and in your name drive out demons and perform many miracles?' if, in fact, we have been 'evildoers' (*Matt. 7:22–23*).

Secondly, we must follow the teaching of Scripture. This is what it means to put to death the misdeeds of the body '*by the Spirit*'. Sometimes we try to do this by other means that are not biblical. Rather than deliver us from sin, they actually drag us deeper and deeper into sin. Paul warns us that it is possible to get caught up in a false mysticism (special 'spiritual' experiences that lift you to a new plane of life in which sin is easily overcome) and a false asceticism (harsh treatment of our bodies and special regulations about food and drink). These do not really transform us inwardly, but instead lead us into deep spiritual bondage (see *Col. 2:1–23*).

By contrast, we are to follow the exhortations of Scripture: whole-hearted obedience to the commandments of the Lord; putting aside the deeds of darkness; clothing ourselves with Christ; refusing to let our minds dwell on the ways in which we can gratify the desires of the flesh (see *Rom. 13:8–14*). Similar teaching is found in Paul's positive exposition of mortification in Colossians 3:1–17.

Thirdly, we must crucify the flesh (*Gal. 5:24*). When we became Christians, we did that in a radical, once-and-for-all way. We put aside the principle of living according to the dictates of the flesh, and instead gave ourselves to the will of the Spirit expressed in God's word.

But we must continue to stand on that high ground of consecration. We need to sow to the Spirit, not the flesh (*Gal. 6:8*); the world must be crucified to us (*Gal. 6:14*). There must be a radical and consistent denial of anything and everything that will draw us away from Christ and from sharing in his holiness. Sin must be refused and starved, not played with and fed. Our instincts, so long under the dominion of the flesh, so long belonging to the old order from which we have been set free by Christ, need to be rigorously retrained for the *new order*. If we have died to sin (which we have), we must no longer live as though we are under its dominion (*Rom. 6:2*).

The third effect of the Spirit of adoption is reproduction. There is a further strand of teaching surrounding what Paul has to say about the presence of the Spirit of adoption in the life of the Christian. The Spirit *reproduces* in our lives the basic pattern that he produced in the life of Jesus.

This pattern appears in Romans 8:11. Paul argues that God will reproduce in us what he accomplished first in Christ, namely resurrection – through the Spirit. Later, Paul tells us that, as God's children, we are heirs with Christ 'if indeed we share in his sufferings in order that we may also share in his glory' (*Rom. 8:17*).

There is an orderliness to the Spirit's purpose in our lives, a pattern of suffering followed by glory. But why this particular pattern and order? Because our sufferings and glory are a share in Christ's. Just as *in order to bring many sons to glory*, Jesus, the pioneer of our salvation, was made perfect through suffering, we are to follow in his footsteps (see *Heb. 2:10*).

What does this mean? We have already seen that, in obedience to the Lord, we are to crucify – to mark with the sign of Christ's death – all our sin and sinful dispositions. The pattern that God has set for us to follow as his children is that crucifying sin will lead to the enjoyment of the new life he has given us.

There is another dimension altogether in which this same pattern of death-producing-life, suffering-leading-to-glory, is employed. It is not simply that *we* are to employ it, thus imitating Christ (cf. *I Pet. 2:21*). God himself brings us through experiences in his sovereign directing of our lives in which he shapes us by suffering and sorrow, by trial and difficulty, *just as he did with his own Son*. Fittingly, Simon Peter (in whose life this pattern was so necessary and so fruitful) expounds this teaching in detail:

Now for a little while you may have had to suffer grief in all kinds of trials. These have come so that your faith – of greater worth than gold, which perishes even though refined by fire – may be proved genuine and may result in praise, glory and honour when Jesus Christ is revealed (*1 Pet. 1:6–7*).

Dear friends, do not be surprised at the painful trial you are suffering, as though something strange were happening to you. But rejoice that you participate in the sufferings of Christ, so that you may be overjoyed when his glory is revealed. If you are insulted because of the name of Christ, you are blessed, for the Spirit of glory and of God rests on you (*1 Pet. 4:12–14*).

And the God of all grace, who called you to his eternal glory in Christ, after you have suffered a little while, will himself restore you and make you strong, firm and steadfast (*1 Pet. 5:10*).

In these passages we see a recurring theme. There is a rhythm, a pattern to our Christian experience: suffering leads to glory; trials lead to victory; hardships are the pathway to maturity. It is, as John Calvin once said, a simple fact that in his family, God has planned that the cross should be the way to victory, death the way to life. It is so for the children of God because it was so for the Son of God. Since we have his own Spirit working in our lives, we can anticipate that the same pattern will be reproduced in order to conform us to the image of our Elder Brother. All this is ours in fellowship with the Spirit of adoption.

Finally, Paul implies that the Spirit of adoption brings a spirit of liberty to the Christian. The Spirit does not bring us into bondage: he brings us into freedom. That freedom has several aspects that will be discussed in later chapters.

Not all Christians enter into their full inheritance. Instead, they quench the Spirit; they experience a sense of restriction rather than a sense of liberty. We constantly need to rediscover that 'where the Spirit of the Lord is, there is freedom' (*2 Cor. 3:17*). The next chapter is devoted to that theme.

7
Family Freedom

One of the great features of the biblical teaching about sonship is its emphasis on the freedom that the sons of God enjoy. We shall see in Chapter Nine that we do not yet enjoy the full liberty of sons. That still awaits us in the presence of God. We may sing about 'full salvation', but the reality of it is yet to dawn on God's children. The liberty for which creation longs – namely, the liberty of the *glory* of the children of God (*Rom. 8:21*) – belongs to the next era of God's redemptive design. In this sense we are still waiting for our final adoption as sons when, with redeemed bodies, we will be able to serve the Lord free from the restrictions of our sinful condition (*Rom. 8:23*).

Although we do not yet experience the liberty of God's glory, we do enjoy the liberty of his *grace*! This present possession of liberty is of central importance in the Christian life. Here we may think of Jesus' great pronouncement: 'If the Son sets you free, you will be free indeed' (*Jn. 8:36*).

The wider context of this statement (*Jn. 8:31–47*) is, in fact, a discussion of family origins. The Jews claimed they possessed Abraham's faith in the promised Messiah. 'The only Father we have is God himself,' they argued (*8:41*). Christ replied, 'If God were your Father, you would love me . . . You belong to your father, the devil' (*8:42–44*). It is in this context that Jesus affirms, 'If the Son sets you free, you will be free indeed' (*8:36*); that is, they would enjoy the freedom of God's true sons. Freedom is, therefore, a hallmark of all genuine faith in Christ, just as loving Christ is the hallmark of true freedom.

Jesus Christ is the great Liberator of men. When, at the commencement of his ministry, he announced the purpose for which God had sent him he added to the following reading from Isaiah these simple words: 'Today this scripture is fulfilled in your hearing':

> The Spirit of the Lord is on me,
>> because he has anointed me
>> to preach good news to the poor.
> He has sent me to proclaim freedom for the
>> prisoners
>> and recovery of sight for the blind,
> to release the oppressed,
>> to proclaim the year of the Lord's favour.
>> (*Lk. 4:18–19*)

What do these words mean? The background to Jesus' proclamation of liberty was the Jewish Year of Jubilee, described in Leviticus 25. In the Old Testament law, the principle of the sabbath was extended beyond one *day* in seven. Every seventh *year* the land was given a sabbath rest when the fields would not be sown nor the vines pruned. Then, after every seven sabbath years (*every fiftieth year*), a 'Great Sabbath Year' was held, the Year of Jubilee. In that year, from the Day of Atonement (in the seventh month of the year), there was to be neither sowing nor reaping. Everyone returned to his own property and slaves were set free. It was to be a year of liberation. It was announced by the blowing of the trumpet everywhere through the land.

Here, in Luke 4, we have our Lord's sounding of the trumpet to announce the year of God's Jubilee. He is saying that the Old Testament law was but a pale shadow of what would now take place in the Messianic reign now inaugurated by the presence of the kingdom of God. The captives were now to be set at liberty through Christ! Jesus' whole ministry is an exposition of what he understood these words to mean. The year of the Lord's favour, the 'today' of which Christ spoke, meant freedom from all kinds of bondage. God wanted his children to be his free sons and daughters.

THE DIMENSIONS OF FREEDOM

The apostle Paul takes up this theme of freedom for God's children in his letter to the Galatians. True Christian freedom was under attack. He therefore re-emphasised what the gospel does in our lives. It allows us to enjoy the full rights of sons because we are no longer slaves (*Gal. 4:6–7*). Now we belong to the Jerusalem above, which is free (*4:26*). In a word, it is for *freedom* that Christ has set us free (*5:1*); it was for freedom that we were called into the family of God (*5:13*).

There are two elements to Paul's description of this freedom.

First, *this freedom is comparative*. In Galatians, Paul is thinking about our freedom as sons in comparison with the relative restrictions of the Old Testament dispensation. The background to what he says is the history of redemption from the time of Moses until the time of Christ and the day of Pentecost. Already he had emphasised that there is only *one* way of salvation; it is received only through Christ. In the Old Testament, believers received it in a promise; in the New Testament, it is received in its fulfilment in Christ. But in both eras, it is the same way of salvation.

Before the coming of Christ, men had only the promise, not the reality. In order to keep them faithful, God gave his people the law (Paul is thinking of the ceremonial and civil restrictions particularly here) to be a *paidagōgos* (*Gal. 3:24*) – the slave whose responsibility it was to take children to school – an apt description, surely! The law, then, was a kind of guardian, restricting life, keeping God's children within narrowly defined bounds *until* the sending of the Son *and* the sending of the Spirit of the Son into our hearts (*4:4,6*).

Through Christ we are redeemed from the curse of the law we have broken, and set free from the special childhood disciplines of the Mosaic law. Through the Spirit we become conscious of our freedom, and in his power we begin to fulfil the commands of the moral law. This is our liberty. By comparison with the Old Testament believer, Paul says we are like sons who have entered into the full rights of our sonship, and are no longer under guardians (*pedagogues*) or trustees (*lawyers*, usually!). The time set by the Father has come (*4:2*); now is the Year of Jubilee for God's people. We are full-grown children! We are free!

Secondly, *this freedom is also substantial*. By comparison with the believer in the Old Testament, we have entered into the full rights of sons. But what is the content of this freedom we enjoy? There are at least seven dimensions to our freedom as sons and daughters of God.

(1) We are free from guilt in order to enjoy peace as God's children. In Romans 8:12ff. Paul provides central teaching on sonship, as we have seen. What is the foundation of this teaching? How can God adopt sinners into his family? How do we know that, having adopted us,

he will not reject us? Our assurance and our peace rest on the fact that our adoption is established on the grounds of our justification.

Since Christ did what the law could not do, namely bear the judgement and condemnation that the law itself pronounced against us as sinners, we know that 'there is now no condemnation for those who are in Christ' (*Rom. 8:1–4*). The word *condemnation* here includes the idea of the prison sentence that follows the judgement of the court. This is a great assurance. Hand in hand with our adoption goes the fact that we are permanently freed from the guilt of sin; we do not need to fear that our presence in the family of God is a temporary measure that may soon come to an end. There is no danger that we will be 'found out' as unworthy of the family. God himself has taken steps to assure us of that. Because we are justified by faith, we have peace with God, and peace with God means freedom from fear, and the enjoyment of the Spirit of adoption (cf. *Rom. 8:15*).

(2) We are free from the reign of sin in order to serve under the reign of Christ. We have already noticed that in Romans 5 and 6 the apostle Paul seems to picture sin in personal terms. He uses the definite article frequently before the word *hamartia* (sin) in those chapters, and literally speaks of *the sin*: sin reigned (*5:21*); it was the *king* in whose kingdom we once lived (*6:2*); it was our *master* (*6:14*), and we were its slaves (*6:16, 20*); it was our *employer*, and paid the wages of death (*6:23*); it was our *general*, and in its service we offered our bodies as weapons (Greek: *hopla*; NIV: 'instruments', *6:13*).

In Christ, however, we have been set free from sin's reign and dominion; because we have died with Christ (*6:2*), we have been freed from sin. We are no longer 'slaves to sin' (*6:6*). And now that we have been set free from sin, we have become slaves of righteousness (*6:18*).

We are no longer children of darkness, but sons of the light (*Eph. 5:8*). We are free to live in the light.

This is a recurring emphasis in the New Testament, and with good reason. There is no more insidious enemy of the enjoyment of the liberty of the sons of God than the suspicion that we are still slaves of our old master. That is why we need to return to this strong biblical teaching over and over again, until we begin to take in the privileges that are ours as co-heirs with Jesus Christ.

(3) We enjoy freedom from the bondage of Satan, in order to enjoy the yoke of Jesus Christ. By nature we are children of wrath, followers of the prince of the power of the air – Satan (*Eph. 2:2–3*). But Christ has broken Satan's hold over us.

How did Christ do so? He bore the sin and guilt that made us subject to the control of Satan. He broke Satan's power on the cross. So Paul teaches when he says that on the cross, Christ disarmed the principalities and powers and made a public example of them (*Col. 2:15*). So, too, says the letter to the Hebrews when it affirms that through his death, Christ disarmed the one who holds the power of death, *in order to free all those who through fear of death were subject to lifelong bondage* (*Heb. 2:14–15*).

John brings this out with remarkable skill and power in his teaching on what it means to be a child of God through new birth. Why did the Son of God come? Specifically to destroy the works of the devil (*1 Jn. 3:8*). What is the practical consequence of this? John's answer is: 'No-one who is born of God will continue to sin, because God's seed remains in him; he cannot go on sinning, because he has been born of God. This is how we know who the children of God are and who the children of the devil are' (*1 Jn. 3:9–10*). Christ overcame Satan on the cross, but the practical repercussions of that become ours only when we are born again into the kingdom of God, and begin to participate in the new liberty of the children of the kingdom.

John takes this even further. We no longer live in sin (the lifestyle of the kingdom of darkness). This is so not only because we have been born again into the family of God, but also because the One who was born of God keeps us. Although the whole world lies in the grip of the Evil One, we enjoy freedom from him; he 'does not touch' us (*1 Jn. 5:18–19*). Since we are under the yoke of Christ (*Matt. 11:29–30*), and bound in his service, he has promised to guard us from temptations that are beyond our endurance (*1 Cor. 10:13*). Would not any elder brother do the same?

(4) We are free from the law in order to live in the Spirit. We need to notice what this does *not* mean. It clearly does not mean that the Christian lives in disregard of the law of God.

The fulfilment of the law is the expression of the love that marks out the children of God: those who are God's children love; those who love keep the commandments (*Jn. 14:15; 15:10, Rom. 13:8–10, 1 Jn. 2:5*). 'This is love for God: to obey his commands.' Freedom does not imply disobedience. Further, 'his commandments are not burdensome' (*1 Jn. 5:3*). Consequently, obedience does not imply a loss of liberty.

How, then, are we free from the law? We are free from its condemnation (*Rom. 8:1*); we are free from its ceremonies, since they find their fulfilment in Christ who offered one sacrifice for sins for all time, and brought to an end the ceremonial offerings of the old covenant when he sat down at the right hand of God (*Heb. 9:24–28*, cf. *10:12–14*).

We are also free from the restrictions of the law. Were it not for the fact that the New Testament itself uses similar language about the Mosaic administration of the law, we would be reticent to speak in these terms. But the New Testament does use such language, in order to emphasise the measure of our freedom. Of course the law is holy, just, and good (*Rom. 7:12*) in its entirety (not simply the Ten Commandments, to which Paul is referring specifically in that verse). But the ceremonial and civil aspects of the law were intended by God as a temporary and typical measure. Although God's *children* lived under those measures, by comparison with the full liberty of the new covenant, the civil and ceremonial aspects could be described as 'slavery' (*Gal. 4:3*).

An everyday example may help us to catch Paul's meaning. Many young people enjoy school; they experience little sense of frustration despite the rigorous time-table by which they live, or even the strictness of the discipline they experience (in some schools, at least). But when they leave school and begin to work, or go to college, where their lives are much more under their own control, what do they discover? By comparison, school seems to have been a form of carefully controlled slavery!

So much is this the case that often (in my time, at least) teachers would warn us about how difficult we might find it to handle our new-found freedom! 'It isn't like school, where you are closely supervised,' they would say. To some of us, perhaps, that close supervision was something we had never noticed; after all, we had no other experience by which to judge school. *Only in the light of our new freedom did we recognise the previous stage as one of strict supervision.*

So it was with the early Christians. They were freed from the restrictions of the Mosaic law. God now said: 'I am no longer giving detailed rules for your life, for the things you touch, for the food you eat. You are a child with full rights. I have given you principles by which to live, and I am giving you the freedom to live wisely by them. Enjoy the freedom I am now giving you.'

Why is our freedom important? To some of us this freedom from the Mosaic law may seem to have little practical relevance. But it is a principle of great significance whenever it is breached (as it frequently was among the early Christians). Then, when someone insists on applying the ceremonial laws or the civil penalties as obligatory and binding on believers today, we need to remind them and ourselves of the stark contrast presented in the New Testament, that emphasises the liberty we have been given by God precisely in these matters.

(5) We enjoy freedom from hypocrisy, freedom to live transparently before the Father. So long as we live before God on the principle that we *earn* his favour, we can never be certain that he loves and accepts us. We can never be sure that we have done *enough* to merit his acceptance. We are driven, therefore, to one of three options. We can seek his mercy. If we do not, we will be driven to despair (How can I *ever* please God?), or we will become hypocrites, pretending that we live lives acceptable to God, all the while knowing that we have fallen short of his commands.

Jesus describes hypocrisy of this kind in the areas of giving (alms), praying, and self-discipline (fasting). He paints three vivid word-pictures of how the hypocrite delights to be honoured by men (*Matt. 6:1–18*). But Jesus does so in the Sermon on the Mount, in which he is describing life in the kingdom of God. He is counselling his disciples that, although they may be tempted to be like the hypocrites, there is a basic principle in the kingdom that delivers them from hypocrisy.

What is this principle that gives so much freedom? Again and again our Lord highlights it. It is the knowledge that God is '*your Father*' (*Matt. 6:1, 4, 6, 8–9, 14–15, 18*). When we know that we are sons of God and have the Spirit of adoption, we long to be obedient to God in every respect, to be faithful and sacrificial in giving, to be earnest in praying, to be regular in self-discipline. But we do all this because God *is already* our Father and because he has *already* accepted us.

To be a child of God is to have true freedom. To *know* that you are a child of God, and to be able to come to him addressing him as 'Father' is the beginning of a life of transparent Christlikeness. That freedom eventually impresses all those who come in contact with it.

(6) We also enjoy freedom from anxiety, which enables us to live *today* for God. 'This is my Father's world,' we sing. Jesus reminds us to let that truth become one of the foundations of our being.

We live in a society that is addicted to anxiety, and, therefore, addicted to possessions, hoping for a certainty that this world cannot provide. So much of life is dominated by the effort to control tomorrow, which is beyond our control. The gospel provides the only remedy for our deep-seated anxieties: this is the world that our Father has made and over which he rules in his perfect wisdom.

'Do not be anxious,' Jesus says. Why not? Because your Father knows what you need and your Father is in control and aware of everything that happens (*Matt. 6:26–27, 32*). It is 'little faith' (children not trusting their Father) that lies at the root of anxiety (*Matt. 6:30*). By contrast, the privilege of the children of God is to have confident faith in the loving-kindness and sufficient provision that their Father has promised to give them.

(7) Finally, we are free from the traditions of men, so that we are bound only by the teaching of God.

One of the reasons we continue to find the teaching of the New Testament so contemporary is because in every age people distort the teaching of the gospel in similar ways. The details may differ (few people would regard themselves as Gnostics or Judaizers today), but the details are simply the packaging. The basic principles that they cover are perennial. So, when Paul speaks of those who were led astray and deceived by teaching that is dependent on human traditions and involves 'fine-sounding arguments' (*Col. 2:4,8*), we may be sure that Christians today will face similar deceptive teaching in one form or another. In this context, too, we need to reaffirm that we are 'free and belong to no man' (*1 Cor. 9:19*).

What is the principle that regulates our freedom? It is that, as God's children, we are bound in conscience to the word our Father has spoken (in Scripture, properly interpreted, *2 Tim. 3:15– 16*). But in all other matters we have freedom to exercise our God-given wisdom and discernment.

These 'other matters' are sometimes described in technical language as the *adiaphora*, or *'things indifferent'*. They constitute a vital area of Christian freedom, but one in which the people of God have often failed to maintain the liberty the Lord has given to them.

The Pharisees were an example of this failure to maintain freedom. We have already seen that the Mosaic law was much more rigorous in its details than the prescriptions of the New Testament. Even so, the Pharisees, who were originally a kind of Old Testament 'higher life' movement, felt that in order to safeguard obedience to God's laws, further laws (human traditions) needed to be added. This had devastating effects, as Jesus saw so clearly. It distorted man's freedom, it distorted the real character of the law, and ultimately it distorted the character of God's grace, and therefore of God himself.

Failure to allow 'things indifferent' to be judged by individual conscience ultimately drove the Pharisees into satanic opposition to the kingdom of God and to Jesus. By their traditions they *nullified* the word of God, said our Lord (*Mk. 7:13*). In this instance, 'things indifferent' could not be treated as a matter of indifference! Jesus had to rebuke the Pharisees and demonstrate the freedom God had given his people under the law (hence, for example, his healings on the sabbath day, in which he demonstrated the difference between what God had intended in his law and the distortion that the Pharisees had created by their traditions).

In a sense, the Pharisees were the 'fundamentalists' of the old covenant church. Unlike the Sadducees (the 'liberals'), the Pharisees believed in Scripture, in the supernatural, in the resurrection, and so on. They were – at least originally – earnest, zealous men. But their failure to grasp the grace of God and the liberty he gives to his people turned them into distorted personalities, men whose hypocrisy masked the true pollution of their hearts. Because of their man-made regulations, they were more concerned with what other men thought of them than with the word of the Lord to them.

You need little imagination to see that the same temptation has often mastered Christians who have taken holiness with equal seriousness, but who have failed to be content with what God says in his word, and – like the Pharisees, in order to be 'safe' – have added non-biblical traditions to the teaching of Scripture. The 'do's and don'ts' of holiness were present also in the New Testament church (*Col. 2:21*).

No one has better expressed where this kind of attitude of following men's traditions can eventually lead than John Calvin:

> The third part of Christian freedom lies in this: regarding outward things that are of themselves 'indifferent,' we are not bound before God by any religious obligation preventing us from sometimes using them and other times not using them, indifferently. And the knowledge of this freedom is very necessary for us, for if

it is lacking, our consciences will have no repose and there will be no end to superstitions . . . these matters are more important than is commonly believed. For when consciences once ensnare themselves, they enter a long and inextricable maze, not easy to get out of. If a man begins to doubt whether he may use linen for sheets, shirts, handkerchiefs, and napkins, he will afterward be uncertain also about hemp; finally, doubt will even arise over tow. For he will turn over in his mind whether he can sup without napkins, or go without a handkerchief. If any man should consider daintier food unlawful, in the end he will not be at peace with God when he eats either black bread or common victuals, while it occurs to him that he could sustain his body on even coarser foods. If he boggles at sweet wine, he will not with clear conscience drink even flat wine, and finally he will not dare touch water if sweeter and cleaner than other water. To sum up, he will come to the point of considering it wrong to step upon a straw across his path, as the saying goes.[1]

Calvin was, perhaps, allowing himself some leeway in describing what actually happens! But the truth he illustrates is, sadly, a reality in many Christians' lives: *The conscience that does not know the freedom of a son before the Father, and is not controlled by the word of the Father, will be in bondage to shibboleths for the whole of life.*

The word *shibboleth* is appropriate in this context. The dictionary defines it as a 'test word or principle or behaviour or opinion, the use of or inability to use which betrays one's party'. It is the Hebrew word for an ear of grain, but its significance is derived from the story in Judges 12, in which it played such a significant part.

[1] John Calvin, *Institutes*, III. xix. 7, ed. J. T. McNeill, trans. F. L. Battles (Philadelphia: Westminster Press, 1960).

The Gileadites were fighting the Ephraimites and had captured the fords of the Jordan River leading to Ephraim. Whenever someone came to cross over the fords, the Gileadites would test them to see whether they were, in fact, Ephraimites. They asked: 'Are you an Ephraimite?' If the answer was 'No', they would add: 'Say "Shibboleth".'

Why did they make such a strange request? Apparently because Ephraimites always pronounced the sound 'sh' as 'ss'. It was rather like a Scot asking a person: 'Are you English?' and if the answer was 'No', testing them by asking: 'Say "loch", then.' If 'loch' was pronounced 'lock' (with a hard ending), the Englishman would immediately be identified! So, at the fords of the Jordan, if a man said 'sibboleth', he was slain.

The word *shibboleth* has come into our vocabulary as a picturesque way of describing practices that have been made acceptable or unacceptable forms of Christian behaviour, which, in fact, are cultural rather than biblical. The point is this: no shibboleth, no distinctive practice that is not taught in Scripture, should ever be made the basis either for fellowship or separation from fellowship among the children of God. *In these matters the children of God have been given liberty by their Father, and they must permit that liberty to be enjoyed by other members of the family.* Sadly, the chief hindrance to our enjoying the liberty of God's sons is sometimes the fact that we are either ignorant of what Scripture teaches, or we lack the discernment to see that certain traditions we have adopted as 'kosher' or certain practices we refrain from adopting as 'sinful', are simply no more than the traditions of men.

But we must now examine a further major element in our treatment of Christian freedom.

THE BOUNDARIES OF FREEDOM

We often fail to enjoy the liberty God has given us; we live narrow, restricted lives, fearful of what other Christians may say or think about us. We can so easily be in bondage to the fear of men (yes, even Christian men).

But the reverse can also be true. We may abuse our God-given freedom. Like the apostle Paul, we also have to fight against errors on the right hand and on the left (*2 Cor. 6:7*) in our daily Christian life. For that reason, Scripture issues words of counsel in two directions.

First, *do not interpret Christian liberty as a licence to sin.* There are repeated warnings for us about this. How can we who have died to sin, and are no longer in its kingdom, go on living in sin? asks Paul (*Rom. 6:1–2*). Yet, apparently there were those (and still are) who say, 'Since God's grace covers our sin, let us go on as we please, and he will continue to forgive us.' What such people fail to realise is that the only freedom we have is *freedom in union with Jesus Christ our Lord.* If we have that freedom, we will exercise it under his Lordship. To exercise freedom in any other way would be to belong to another master. We are to live as free men, and not to use that freedom as a cover-up for our sin (*1 Pet. 2:16*).

The principle is this: 'You, my brothers, were called to be free. But do not use your freedom to indulge the sinful nature [the flesh]; rather, serve one another in love' (*Gal. 5:13*). Thus, we are to use our freedom for loving others.

The second direction in which Scripture counsels us is, *do not exercise your Christian liberty in a spirit of indifference to your brothers in Christ.* This was an issue in at least two of the New Testament letters, and is a recurring problem in the family of God.

In Corinth some of the Christians had placed great stress on the new freedom the gospel brought to them, and the way in which their spirits had been liberated in the worship of God. In some cases they carried their freedom to excess. ('What is the importance of "decency" when you have the liberty of the Spirit?') But Paul stresses that things should be done 'in a fitting and orderly way' (*1 Cor. 14:40*), because God is a God of order (*14:33*). Paul responded to this situation in a series of questions by which the Corinthians – and we, too – might regulate the proper use of Christian liberty.

(1) 'Is the exercise of my liberty proving to be beneficial to me?' (*1 Cor. 6:12; 10:23*). It may be true, Paul argues, that everything is permissible for me, because I am free in Jesus Christ. But my freedom is never the only principle for my actions. I also need to ask whether exercising my freedom will enable me to grow in grace and draw nearer to the Lord. Not everything that is lawful is necessarily beneficial *to me*.

(2) 'Is the exercise of my freedom contributing to the growth and blessing of others?' (*1 Cor. 10:23–24*). How easily we confuse freedom with the number of rights we are able to possess. But true Christian freedom does not consist of the increase of 'my rights'. It consists of service! Consequently, Christ's freemen are willing to deny themselves the exercise of their 'rights' in order to contribute to the growth of others. In fact, the only men and women who are truly free are those who are free from their supposed 'rights' and are able to exercise them or not with relative indifference.

(3) 'Is the desire to exercise my freedom actually proving to be a snare to me?' (*1 Cor. 6:12*). Sadly, it is all too common for Christians to become enslaved to the freedoms about which they boast. We lose sight of the importance of keeping ourselves in subjection (*9:24–27*). We forget that we are sinners who can easily pervert liberty into licence. The brother who *boasts* to his 'weaker'

brother that he is free to drink whatever he chooses may, sadly, be the man who is enslaved to his supposed 'freedom'. His drinking proves to be bondage because he has boasted in his strength, and has forgotten that he is still a sinner, albeit saved by grace.

If only the Corinthians had regulated the use of their liberty by these principles, all would have been well! But, unlike Paul, they were not prepared to 'put up with anything rather than hinder the gospel of Christ' (*9:12*).

In the church at Rome (perhaps among the various congregations spread throughout the city) there seem to have developed different groups with different practices – indeed, different shibboleths. Paul speaks of them in two categories (probably those used by one faction, rather than invented by Paul himself). They were 'the weak' and 'the strong'. Their differences revolved around matters of conscience involving the use of certain food and drink, and the status of particular days. Were Christians forbidden to eat certain kinds of food, and should they regard some days as holier than others?

The strong believed they could eat anything, drink anything, and use all days alike. The weak, by contrast, believed that it would be sinful to eat certain foods, drink certain beverages, and treat all days alike. Of course, perhaps not all the weak held to all of these restrictions on their liberty.

Two things should stand out for us in this situation. The first is the subtle change that has taken place in our use of words and categories. In Rome the strong were those who felt free to eat and drink and use all days alike. Today Christians who have scruples in these different areas (or others, for that matter) tend to regard themselves as having *strong* consciences, and regard those who exercise freedom as having *weak* consciences. That subtle change of vocabulary may be very instructive. But a genuinely strong conscience is not one bound to man-made traditions, but set free from them by the teaching of Scripture.

More important than designations is the reality of the situation. Think for a moment of the potential for destruction in the churches at Rome. How would you cope with the following groups in your church: the pro-meat, drink, and days party; the pro-meat, anti-drink, and pro-days party; the anti-meat, drink, and days party; and the anti-meat and drink, but pro-days party(!)? Of course we can speak of these things with tongue in cheek, but as a matter of fact, most Christians have run into the twentieth-century version of this problem at some time or another. Its potential to destroy churches and fellow-ship is incalculable.

How does Paul deal with this situation? First, he appeals to them *all* as *brothers*. The recognition that they are such, that they belong to the same family, that they have the same Father, lays the proper foundation for them to respond to one another in a truly family way (*Rom. 14:10*). In doing so, Paul actually seems to identify himself with the strong: 'As one who is in the Lord Jesus, I am fully convinced that no food is unclean in itself' (*Rom. 14:14*); 'we who are strong' (*15:1*).

But he also recognises that 'if anyone regards some-thing as unclean, then for him it is unclean' (*Rom. 14:14*). Elsewhere he insists that it is a basic principle of the body of Christ that our freedom should not be judged by another man's conscience (*1 Cor. 10:29*).

None of this meant that Paul (or we) can be indifferent to the promptings of another brother's conscience. So Paul gives the Romans (and us) a series of practical principles to guide us in the use of our freedom. The more important ones can be summarised in five pro-positions.

(1) *We are to welcome all those whom Christ has welcomed without reservation, and without any desire to make these 'indifferent' matters the basis of our fellowship.* This is Paul's first and last word on the matter. We are to 'accept him whose faith is weak, without passing judgment on disputable matters' (*Rom. 14:1*). We are to welcome one another as Christ has welcomed us (*15:7*). Paul presses this point home: Christ, born of the seed of David (a *Jew!*), born as he was under the law, died in order that the *Gentiles* might glorify God for his mercy (*15:8–9*).

(2) *We are to recognise that we stand or fall to our own Master, Christ, and not to one another.* Each one of us will stand before God's judgement seat to give an account of ourselves to the Lord (*14:10, 12*). We will not be judged on the basis of our brother's way of life, or on the basis of what his conscience compelled him to do. On that day, we will stand alone. What is the implication? 'Therefore let us stop passing judgement on one another' (*14:13*).

(3) *We are to resolve not to become a stumbling-block to our brother.* 'Make up your mind not to put any stumbling-block or obstacle in your brother's way' (*14:13*). Perhaps the instinctive response of some members of the church in Rome would have been: 'Why should we restrict our exercise of liberty?' Paul provides the most convincing of answers. It is faith that gives us liberty in Christ (*14:14*). But faith works by love (*Gal. 5:6*). So then, 'If your brother is distressed because of what you eat, you are no longer acting in love' (*Rom. 14:15*).

Furthermore, Christ died for your brother (*Rom. 14:15*). To despise him, even with his weak faith and restricted liberty, is to destroy a brother for whom Christ died. In any case, the kingdom of God does not consist in meat and drink, Paul adds. It is righteousness, peace, and joy in the Holy Spirit. If we regard food and drink (and some particular food and drink, at that) as essentials to our liberty, then we have little comprehension of what it means to seek first the kingdom of God and his righteousness.

(4) *We are to make peace and mutual building-up the aim of our exercise of liberty.* 'Let us therefore make every effort to do what leads to peace and to mutual edification' (*14:19*). Again Paul provides a powerful reason and incentive for this goal. The church is 'the work of God' (*14:20*). Should such a work be destroyed for the sake of food? The growth of the family is far more important than the exercise of my individual freedom of conscience.

(5) *We are to realise that we do not need to exercise our liberty in order to possess it.* Paul hints at the value of self-control when he tells the Romans to keep what they believe about personal preferences in indifferent matters between themselves and God (*14:22*). After all, Christ did not live to please himself (*15:3*). Who do we think we are in the body of Christ if we insist on the exercise of our rights?

When we have reached the point at which we 'need' to exercise our freedom, the question arises whether we have become enslaved to the very thing we thought of as our freedom. In 'matters indifferent' (not matters essential), we should strive for a healthy indifference as to whether we exercise our liberties or not.

There is an interesting example of this principle of self-controlled freedom in the New Testament. Timothy and Titus were two of Paul's helpers in the ministry. Neither had been circumcised as a child. Where the principle of the gospel was at stake, Paul apparently did everything in his power to see that Titus remained uncircumcised. But where the gospel was not at stake, in the case of Timothy, a half-Jew, Paul felt free to have him circumcised in order to further his ministry among the Jews (compare *Acts 16:3* with *Gal. 2:2–5*).

Calvin puts it well: We temper our freedom for the weakness of ignorant believers, but not for the rigour of the Pharisees.[2] Martin Luther expressed the true biblical position even more eloquently when he wrote: 'A Christian is a free lord of all, subject to none: a Christian is a perfectly dutiful servant of all, subject to all.'[3]

We often struggle to maintain such a delicate balance. We can do so only as our minds are increasingly instructed in, and our spirits increasingly sensitive to, the teaching of Scripture. We have to battle to enjoy liberty! But we do so in the assurance that the day will dawn when the liberty of the experience of grace will lead to the full light of the liberty of glory (*Rom. 8:21*).

[2]Ibid., III. xix. 11.
[3]Martin Luther, *Martin Luther's Treatise on Christian Liberty*, trans. W. A. Lambert and H. J. Grimm, in *Three Treatises* (Philadelphia: Fortress Press, 1970), p. 261.

8
Fatherly Discipline

We have seen several dimensions to the way in which we grow as children of God. As the family likeness develops in us, we need to put aside habits and characteristics that are inconsistent with God's overall intention in our lives. But there is another aspect to God's ways, on occasions a painful one: God disciplines us as his children. The classic biblical passage on this theme is Hebrews 12:5–13:

> [5]You have forgotten that word of encouragement that addresses you as sons:
>> 'My son, do not make light of the
>>> Lord's discipline,
>> and do not lose heart when he
>>> rebukes you,
>> [6]because the Lord disciplines those whom he
>>> loves,
>> and punishes everyone he
>>> accepts as a son.'
> [7]Endure hardship as discipline; God is treating you as sons. For what son is not disciplined by his father? [8]If you are not disciplined (and everyone undergoes

discipline), then you are illegitimate children and not true sons. ⁹Moreover, we have all had human fathers who disciplined us and we respected them for it. How much more should we submit to the Father of our spirits and live! ¹⁰Our fathers disciplined us for a little while as they thought best; but God disciplines us for our good, that we may share in his holiness. ¹¹No discipline seems pleasant at the time, but painful. Later on, however, it produces a harvest of righteousness and peace for those who have been trained by it.

¹²Therefore, strengthen your feeble arms and weak knees.¹³ 'Make level paths for your feet,' so that the lame may not be disabled, but rather healed.

The general thrust of this teaching is clear: fathers discipline their children; so, too, the heavenly Father disciplines his children. In explaining this principle, the writer of Hebrews gathers together all of the fundamental biblical teaching on the subject of the discipline that the children of God experience.

THE NECESSITY OF DISCIPLINE

Being disciplined is a mark of legitimacy. It is evidence that our father cares for us. He thinks of ways in which he can mould us into the kind of mature children he wants us to be. So, too, in the realm of the spirit. It is essential for us to be disciplined by our heavenly Father.

Why does Hebrews emphasise discipline? Simply because those early Christians (and we with them) were in danger of *forgetting* such an elementary factor in Christian experience (*Heb. 12:5*). That may seem incomprehensible in the light of the suffering the Hebrew Christians had already endured (see *10:32–34*). But, it is true to human experience. We are often surprised, even disoriented, by the fact that there are painful disciplines in our pilgrimage. We move on to a new stage in our lives when, mistakenly, we expect that trials like those we experienced before will be a thing of the past. But God does not so deal with us.

What has happened when we lose sight of the fact that discipline constitutes a staple ingredient in the Christian life? 'You have forgotten Scripture,' writes the author of Hebrews. 'You have forgotten that word of encouragement that addresses you as sons' (*12:5*). In some cases, perhaps, we could take these words even further: we have been *ignorant* of Scripture. But if we are any distance along the road in spiritual growth, we surely know that Scripture teaches we are on a path of discipleship; we are climbing what John Bunyan aptly called 'the Hill Difficulty'. Yet, how true to life to suggest that we forget! We need to be reminded regularly of the pattern of the Christian life. It involves being disciplined.

This fact could be very discouraging to God's children. But Hebrews tells us that Scripture speaks to us about the discipline and chastisement of our experience for 'encouragement'.

How does this encourage us? The knowledge that God disciplines *all* of his true sons helps *us* to bear his discipline when we receive it. It is evidence to us of God's care, of his interest in us, of his desire for us to grow in grace. Were it not for the teaching of Scripture, our trials might lead us to conclude that God is against us. But the reverse is true. He is, as a Father, working all things together 'for the good of those who love him, who have been called according to his purpose' (*Rom. 8:28*)!

THE NATURE OF DISCIPLINE

Spiritual discipline is not easy to welcome unless we see the Father's hand in it. It involves hardship (*Heb. 12:7*); it is unpleasant and painful (*12:11*). We need only reflect on the disciplining we experienced at the hands of our earthly fathers! There are indeed times when the Lord 'whips' his children (*12:6*).

God uses great variety in his spiritual disciplining. Like the farmer, he ploughs and he sows; he deals differently with different children in order to produce the appropriate harvest of grace.

> When a farmer ploughs for planting, does he
>   plough continually?
>   Does he keep on breaking up and
>   harrowing the soil?
> When he has levelled the surface,
>   does he not sow caraway and scatter
>   cummin?
> Does he not plant wheat in its place,
>   barley in its plot,
>   and spelt in its field?
> His God instructs him
>   and teaches him the right way.
>
> Caraway is not threshed with a sledge,
>   nor is a cartwheel rolled over cummin;
> caraway is beaten out with a rod,
>   and cummin with a stick.
> Grain must be ground to make bread;
>   so one does not go on threshing it for ever.
> Though he drives the wheels of his threshing-
>   cart over it,
>   his horses do not grind it.
> All this also comes from the LORD Almighty,
>   wonderful in counsel and magnificent
>   in wisdom.
>
>   (*Is. 28:24–29*)

How, then, in particular terms does God discipline and chastise his children? What different principles can we trace in the teaching and example of Scripture that we can apply practically to our own lives?

First, *in Scripture we have the words of the Father*. God rebukes us and chastens us through what he says to us in Scripture. This is one of its chief functions, since it is 'God-breathed and is useful for . . . *rebuking*' (*2 Tim. 3:16*).

Rebuking is also one of the ministries of the servants of God's word: 'Preach the Word . . . *rebuke*' (*2 Tim. 4:2*). It is vital for those who are thus servants of the word to remember that this is what they are – *servants*, both of the word of God and of the people of God. It is ultimately only the word of the Lord that rebukes us, not the words of any man. This needs to be underlined. But when we understand that, we should also be grateful for the wise way in which God uses others to discipline us through their faithful application of his word. He instructs our minds and touches our consciences through it, appealing to us to recognise that we have gone out of the way, and to repent and return to him.

How can we best benefit from this avenue of spiritual discipline? There are two things we should do. The first is to place our lives under the influence of the ministry of God's word.

We live in an 'instant' age, when people have become impatient with and uncomfortable under disciplines that take time and regular exercise. We can, therefore, be very easily tempted to despise the fundamental way in which God addresses us and wants to mould our lives, namely, through the patient explanation and application of his living word. The unfolding of God's word brings light, and we have to learn to give our minds and hearts to it wherever we can find it unfolded.

In true preaching, God deals with us as his children; by his Spirit he applies the general principles of Scripture to us individually; he counsels us in private and secret ways that go far beyond any help and wisdom a human counsellor could give to us.

One of the church's greatest needs today is for this kind of ministry. One of our primary personal needs is for this kind of ministry. It is not necessarily spectacular (although it can be): it is long-term; it requires patience and the use of our minds; it calls for serious intentions and persevering decisions. But through it we receive the Lord's discipline.[1]

Next to preaching is our own reading of Scripture. Why place hearing it preached *before* reading it, as though that were more important? Because, in one sense it is. Most of us never rise above reading Scripture the way we hear it expounded. That is simply a fact of human experience. It is the reason James tells us that teachers will be more severely judged (*Jas. 3:1*). But that is not to reduce the vital place personal Bible study should play in our own lives. Through our own reading of Scripture, God addresses us as sons (notice the present tense, *Heb. 12:5*). We sit at our Father's feet, and we listen.

Secondly, *the hand of the Father applies discipline*. God's word is not the only means of discipline he uses, although it is the one he prefers to use. There are times when he resorts to other measures.

Think of Simon Peter. Jesus had called him into the family of God. Yet there was much in Peter's life that needed severe discipline. Our Lord's first method was to use his word. Several times in the Gospels we find Jesus rebuking Peter, endeavouring to discipline his mind through the exposition of truth. In particular, Jesus' teaching related to Peter's failure to grasp the centrality of

---

[1]See the challenging words of John White on this theme in *Flirting with the World: A Challenge to Loyalty* (London: Hodder and Stoughton, 1983), pp. 127ff.

Christ's suffering and the consequent sufferings of those who were his disciples. Peter had no desire to 'endure hardship as discipline' (*Heb. 12:7*).

Then there was Peter's pride and mistaken sense of self-sufficiency. Again Jesus addressed Peter in different ways, to bring him to a new level of maturity through his teaching, and through verbal rebukes (see *Mk. 8:31–38; 14:27–31, Jn. 13:1–7; 21:15–23*). But in Peter's case, verbal rebuke needed to be accompanied by actual chastisement. Peter was 'whipped' (*Heb. 12:6*, literal translation).

God used the most unlikely instruments: a servant girl and a cock crowing in the early hours of morning. These became the means by which Peter was humbled under the mighty hand of God (*1 Pet. 5:6*). The function of those experiences that left deep marks on his whole life and personality was to make him the kind of child of God that Christ wanted him to be. There is more to discipline than the word of the Father. Peter experienced the Father's hand too!

The expression 'the hand of the Lord' is a common one in the Old Testament. It is a picturesque way of describing the practical outworking of God's will and purpose. Just as our hands put into action our own plans, so it is with God. Just as our earthly fathers use their hands to discipline us, so being spiritually disciplined is the work of the hand of the Lord.

God's hand contains various means of discipline. Sometimes he uses periods of sickness. Paul alludes to this in 1 Corinthians 11 in the context of his teaching about the Lord's Supper: 'Many among you are weak and sick, and a number of you have fallen asleep . . . *We are being disciplined* so that we will not be condemned with the world' (*1 Cor. 11:30–32*). We are meant *to learn* through times of sickness. The Psalms bear witness to many of the lessons that can be learned (for example, *Ps. 102*).

Pain can be our teacher. It can teach us the nature of the world in which we live, broken and marred as it is by sin. We often forget that. We fail to live with our possessions held lightly in our hands, as Paul urges us to do (*1 Cor. 7:29–31*). Loneliness, often induced by illness, impresses upon us the need to have communion with God himself as the fundamental possession in our lives. Through this we have been disciplined to see everything more clearly, in the light of eternity.

Through his suffering Paul learned several vital lessons. He was taught that our own solutions to situations must yield to God's better ones. Paul wanted relief from his suffering; God gave him grace to endure his suffering. Paul learned that Christ's strength encamps on his children's weakness. He learned 'when I am weak, then I am strong' (*2 Cor. 12:10*). We often forget that Paul saw a yet more fundamental purpose in the way in which God's hand was on his life: 'to keep me from becoming conceited' (*12:7*). Humility was a fruit of suffering and illness in his case.

God uses tribulation in our lives for his purpose. Our English word *tribulation* is derived from the Latin word *tribulum*, the instrument used in the ancient world to thresh corn. The word that is used in New Testament Greek is equally evocative: *thlipsis*, which means 'pressure'. It is by pressure, of whatever sort, that God creates character in his children's lives. This tribulation, or suffering, 'produces perseverance; perseverance, character; and character, hope' (*Rom. 5:3–4*).

God applies this pressure in many different ways, sometimes so mysterious that it is completely beyond our understanding. Think of the way in which Jesus led his disciples to experience a fierce storm on the Sea of Galilee, so that they cried out: 'Teacher, don't you care if we drown?' (*Mk. 4:38*). His purpose was to reveal to them their fear emerging from their lack of faith, and then to demonstrate to them that he was Master of every situation, every conceivable crisis in life. It was painful discipline; humanly speaking, it involved the most immense risks. But through it the disciples learned lessons they otherwise would never have received.

We can take Joseph as another example. Destined by God to be mightily used, given indications early in life that God had a purpose for him, Joseph – if not actually proud – was at least naive in the way he related his dreams to his family (*Gen. 37:2–11*). He required discipline. The discipline he received was of the most painful kind. Here was somebody whom God 'scourged'! Rejected by brothers, sold as a slave, imprisoned for his righteous rejection of Potiphar's wife, forgotten by those he helped (*Gen. 39–40*), he was able to look back on all of these experiences and say: 'God intended it for good to accomplish what is now being done, the saving of many lives' (*50:20*).

Joseph saw apparently tragic and unjust events in his life in a very different light from that of human judgement: 'God sent me ahead of you . . . to preserve for you a remnant on earth and to save your lives by a great deliverance. So then, it was not you who sent me here, but God. He made me father to Pharaoh . . . God has made me lord of all Egypt' (*45:5–9*). His sufferings were the means by which he was brought to the sphere in which God intended to use him so widely. But they were also the means by which God prepared him to be the kind of man he wanted him to be when his time came! These are the two dimensions in which God works in his children's lives – the level of their service, and the level of their character. That is why, as sons as well as servants, we can say:

As the eyes of slaves look to the hand of their
    master,
  as the eyes of a maid look to the hand of
    her mistress,
so our eyes look to the LORD our God,
  till he shows us his mercy.

(*Ps. 123:2*)

There is a third instrument by which God disciplines his children. Such is the sovereign control of God that *he is able to use even Satan, his own enemy,* to discipline his children. When Jesus described the principles of God's work in the lives of his people, he used the analogy of the Father as a vine-dresser pruning the branches of the vine in order to produce a rich harvest. Every fruitful branch is trimmed in order to be 'even more fruitful' (*Jn. 15:2*). In commenting on these verses in John 15, Martin Luther wrote that the Father says:

> Devil, you are indeed a murderer and an evildoer; but I will use you for my purpose. You shall be My hoe; the world and your following shall be My manure for the fertilization of My vineyard.[2]

Perhaps only Luther would dare to think of the devil as God's 'hoe' to bring his children to new levels of spiritual development. But the general principle is clearly illustrated elsewhere in Scripture. Paul explicitly says: 'There was given me a thorn in my flesh, a messenger of Satan' (*2 Cor. 12:7*); that is, given to him in the providence of God. Satan was seeking to destroy Paul's faith and his testimony, but God had a greater purpose in view by allowing Satan to afflict the apostle. It was through what Satan was doing that God was teaching Paul lessons about his grace.

[2]*Luther's Works*, ed. J. Pelikan, volume 24 (St. Louis: Concordia Publishing House, 1961), p. 195.

The same kind of experience appears in the life of the disciples. Toward the end of his ministry, Jesus explained to them that Satan had demanded to have them in order to sift them like wheat. Jesus told Peter in particular that he had prayed that his faith would not fail (*Lk. 22:31–32*). In fact, the net result of the harrowing of Simon Peter was that he would one day strengthen his fellow disciples.

The pattern is similar in the experience of Job. Satan demanded to have him also, to sift him like wheat and to prove that underneath his profession of loyalty to the Lord there was a *quid pro quo* (something for something) attitude (*Job 1:9–11*). Satan accused Job of being loyal to the Lord for what he could get out of him. God permitted Satan to attack his dear servant, confident that Job would emerge not only as victor, but also as a man refined by sufferings and all the more dedicated to the will of God. And so it proved to be, despite the failures and sins of Job's life (see Job 42).

Jesus' life illustrates the extraordinary lengths to which God is prepared to go in dealing with us. Jesus was led into the wilderness by the Holy Spirit in order to be tempted by the devil (*Lk. 4:1–2*). Here the Spirit's leading and the devil's temptation coincided so that our Lord might be all that God intended him to become as our Saviour. No wonder Paul exclaims: 'Oh, the depth of the riches of the wisdom and knowledge of God! How unsearchable his judgments, and his paths beyond tracing out! Who has known the mind of the Lord? Or who has been his counsellor?' (*Rom. 11:33–34*).

THE FUNCTION OF DISCIPLINE

In considering both the necessity and nature of discipline, we have already noted some aspects of its function. Hebrews 12:5–13 focuses attention specifically on several

important elements. 'God disciplines us for our good.'
What does this mean? Our good is, very specifically,
defined as holiness, and 'a harvest of righteousness'
(*12:10–11*). It is in this sense that when we 'submit to the
Father of our spirits' we shall live (*12:9*). Discipline is
intended to produce holiness of life and character – a
quality of life that is pleasing to God, because it shares in
his own holy nature.

This should be both illuminating and challenging to us:
illuminating because unless we see the ultimate reason for
chastisement and the various painful disciplines of the
Christian life, we will find them extremely difficult to
accept; challenging because unless we share the purposes
God is fulfilling, we shall constantly wriggle under the
painful experiences that come our way. *If we do not value
holiness, we will not welcome discipline.* We will not be able
to 'count it all joy when we suffer various trials', because
our hearts will be set on very different goals from the
perseverance and maturity God is seeking to establish in
our lives (see *Jas. 1:2–4*).

A disciplined life is one in which we learn to exercise
self-control. But it is more than that. It is a life that bears
the marks of God's workmanship, and carries the auto-
graph by which his possessions and handiwork are always
recognised: 'HOLY TO THE LORD' (*Ex. 28:36, Zech.
14:20–21, 1 Pet. 1:15*). That is why those who have
received the Lord's discipline show themselves to be his
true disciples by the character and quality of their lives.
They are 'godly', that is, God-like, because they have been
disciplined in order that they may share in God's holiness
(*Heb. 12:10*).

Here, then, is the divine touchstone by which we are to
regulate all our thinking and living. Whenever the hand of
the Lord touches our lives in discipline, we should not ask
bitterly, 'Why did this happen to me? What could I have

done?' but, 'For what purpose is the Lord now working in my life? In what ways can I respond to the call of God, evident in this experience, to be holy as he, my Father in Heaven, is holy?' In pursuing the answers to these questions, our lives will produce a harvest of righteousness and peace because we have been trained through discipline.

We should, in the meantime, always remember that discipline is *training*. It looks to the future. God is a farmer who ploughs up our hearts in preparation for the harvest; but he is also a sports coach who sees our potential fitness in his service. This is a great reason for encouragement: while the discipline is painful, it is temporary. It also serves as a reminder that discipline belongs to this life only, as John Owen wisely wrote: 'There is no chastisement in heaven, nor in hell. Not in heaven, because there is no sin; not in hell, because there is no amendment.'[3] We ought, then, to value the privileges of the present disciplines that are ours from the hand of God, and yield to their function in our lives.

OUR RESPONSE TO DISCIPLINE

Discipline is not pleasant, but painful. The fact that it has a purpose enables us to endure it, even welcome it, not for its pain but because of the fruit that it will produce in our lives. But because it remains painful we are tempted to respond to it in the wrong way, as the writer of Proverbs 3:11–12 (quoted in *Heb. 12:5–6*) saw very clearly.

We may be tempted to treat discipline lightly. Perhaps that is the leading tendency of our times. Some of our forefathers were sensitive, perhaps over-sensitive, to the chastising hand of God. We have gone to the opposite

[3]John Owen, *Works*, vol. XXIV, p.260.

extreme. Whereas they sometimes felt every misfortune was due to some specific sin, we have become enamoured with a god created by modern psychology, who would never dream of causing pain to his children, even with the best motives. So, although we smart under the pains of life, we shrug off the suggestion that this might be the hand of our Father chastising us. In short, we have made a god in our own image, a god who lacks the seriousness to discipline his children effectively. But that is simply a reflection of our own lack of seriousness with God and his dealings with us. Treating discipline lightly is the action of a fool, according to the wise man (see *Prov. 1:7*). A true son will want to see what his Father is teaching him by the pain of chastisement.

On the other hand, *we may be depressed by discipline*. It can produce a reaction in us of losing heart (*Heb. 12:5*). How does this happen? Ultimately, it has the same cause as treating God's discipline too lightly.

How can this be, when such depression usually occurs in those who appear to take his disciplines with much greater seriousness?

Losing heart under discipline is a fruit of lack of faith and understanding. The depressed spirit sees only suffering, pain, and unpleasantness in discipline. It does not see the Father's hand, his purpose, and the ultimate goal of holiness and Christlikeness. It has also forgotten the word of encouragement that addresses us as sons (*Heb. 12:5*)!

In some Christian circles, that spirit of heaviness and of depression is seen as a sign of spirituality. But it is nothing of the kind. It is a deep-rooted failure to come to terms with God's Fatherly sovereignty over our lives.

How, then, are we to respond biblically to God's disciplines? In a word, we are to *submit* to them. If we had human fathers who disciplined us and we respected them for doing so, 'how much more should we submit to the

Father of our spirits and live!' (*Heb. 12:9*). We submit in the recognition of what God is doing in our lives (working for our good, creating in us his holiness, producing the peaceable fruits of righteousness, *12:11*), and in doing so, we discover that God works out his will with perfect judgement and timing.

Through their submission to discipline, the lame, rather than being disabled, are healed. Setting a dislocated limb may seem to be a painful experience, but it is a healing act. To an untrained, inexperienced observer, it might seem to be an act of uncaring brutality. But to the person who is experiencing the pain, who realises the motives of his physician and trusts him, it is the first step back to health and strength. So our attitude to the Lord's disciplines will be: 'Strengthen your feeble arms and weak knees! "Make level paths for your feet," so that the lame may not be disabled, but rather healed' (*Heb. 12:12–13*).

9
The Final Destiny

We must now try to put our study of the biblical teaching on being a child of God in its ultimate perspective.

God's pattern of dealing with men has always been determined by the model of sonship. Adam was his son, and when he sinned and fell, God worked in history in order to call his son, Israel, out of Egypt. That relationship (which in Romans 9:4 the New Testament calls *adoption*) was intended to be a shadow of the full reality of sonship that would come through Jesus Christ. Before his coming, men were sons of God through faith. But they were sons under age, who experienced the restrictions of the legal dispensation of the old covenant. Now, in Christ, we enter into a new stage of experiencing God as our Father through the new covenant.

There are other parallels between the revelation of the old and new covenants. Under the old, God's son, Israel, was promised an inheritance. Until God's true heir, Christ, was born, that inheritance was expressed in a very physical nature, by possession of the land of Canaan (cf. *Ex. 15:17*, *1 Chron. 16:18*, *Ps. 105:11*). There was one interesting exception to that principle. Aaron and his descendants were to have no inheritance in the land; their inheritance was to be the Lord himself! (See Deut. 18:1–2) The priestly family served as a constant reminder that the ultimate fulfilment of God's promised inheritance was not to be found geographically, in the land, but spiritually, in Christ and his presence with his people.

This teaching is carried over into the New Testament. We are the children of God; we, therefore, receive an inheritance from him. Our final destiny is to enter into the full enjoyment of that inheritance.

Peter emphasises our inheritance when he speaks about the blessings of regeneration. We have been born again to receive an inheritance from God, which can never fade away (*I Pet. 1:3–4*). In a similar way, Paul speaks of the inheritance in connection with adoption. If we are adopted children, he argues, it follows that we are heirs of God and joint-heirs with Christ – provided we suffer with him, in order that we may be glorified together with him (*Rom. 8:17*). Since we are children, God has also made us heirs (*Gal. 4:7*).

Inheritance, therefore, is a central element in the teaching of the New Testament. It has both a present and a future element. We have already seen that we are no longer slaves, but sons, freedmen in the household of God. We are no longer under the restrictions imposed by the Mosaic law. Yet, obviously, we have not yet reached the point where all the fullness of the blessings of our inheritance are ours. Here, as in all areas of Christian experience, there is a tension between what we *already* experience and what we do *not yet* experience.

Recognising this tension is fundamental to understanding biblical teaching on what it means to be a Christian and a child of God. John says basically the same thing when he reminds us: 'Now we *are* children of God, and what we *will be* has not yet been made known' (*1 Jn. 3:2*). In other words, although the privilege of being a Christian is glorious, there is yet more to experience!

Paul describes our destiny, and its present significance like this: '*Those God foreknew he also predestined to be conformed to the likeness of his Son, that he might be the firstborn among many brothers*' (*Rom. 8:29*). Five key words summarise Paul's teaching.

1. *Likeness*. What is the 'likeness' of Christ? *Likeness* and *image* are very important words in biblical theology. We earlier noted that man was originally made in the image and likeness of God (*Gen. 1:26–27*). He was made to reflect the glory of God in a unique way. But he sinned, and his descendants were made in *his* image, the image of a fallen creature, in whom the image of the glory of God was distorted (*Gen. 5:3*). Man exchanged the glory of God for the worship of the creature; he fell from the glory of God (*Rom. 1:21–23; 3:23*). In the created order the glory of God (which even the heavens proclaim – *Ps. 19:1*) is no longer reflected in a personal being. This is the tragedy of man, who was destined to be God's son; the image, the likeness, the glory of the One who created him has been marred – sometimes, it seems, almost beyond recognition.

God has not been content to leave things there, as we have seen. He brought a new son, the nation of Israel, into being in the Exodus. God's cloud of glory, his shekinah-presence, rested again on his son, as though he were giving the world a momentary glimpse of what he had originally intended, and unveiling his intentions for the future.

Then God sent his Son, Jesus. He is the heir of all things, the one through whom the universe was brought into being. He is also 'the radiance of God's glory and the exact representation of his being' (*Heb. 1:3*). *He* took our human nature, so that in our flesh he might repair the image and glory of God. When men of faith saw him, they were impressed by 'his glory, the glory of the one and only Son, who came from the Father, full of grace and truth' (*Jn. 1:14*). His ultimate purpose in coming was to be the firstborn of the many brothers who will one day reflect all that God intended man to be. God's children will one day share the image of his one and only Son, Jesus (*1 Cor. 15:49*). That is the work in which God is engaged.

2. *Restoration*. Restoration is an excellent way in which to describe what the Father is doing. Think for a moment of some great man whose life has been ruined by addiction. He has gambled away his resources; he has drunk away his senses; his family has abandoned him; his bedraggled appearance betrays the fact that his only home is old, uninhabited buildings. Yet, when he speaks, there is a reminder of the home, the breeding, the education he once had. But he is incapable of bringing himself back to the original status. The marks of his former dignity remain, but only underline the tragedy of his present condition. So it is with man. The wonder of the gospel is that God has restoration plans.

We should not be surprised to discover that when God makes sons out of derelicts, the work of restoration may be slow, difficult, and even painful to us. Habits are ingrained in us that are an affront to the Father. We have lived, perhaps for years, with tendencies that are contrary to his will. In many ways we might more easily become a 'hired servant' as the first prodigal son imagined he would be (*Lk. 15:19*). In some ways life would be a lot easier!

But God will make us nothing less than sons! He will not be satisfied by anything short of the restoration of his own image and the reflection of his own glory in our lives. He does not want hired servants (he has angels enough!); he wants children. C. S. Lewis admirably expressed this when he wrote:

Imagine yourself as a living house. God comes in to rebuild that house. At first, perhaps, you understand what He is doing. He is getting the drains right, and stopping the leaks in the roof, and so on: you knew that those jobs needed doing and you are not surprised. But presently He starts knocking the house about in a way that hurts abominably, and does not seem to make sense. What on earth is He up to? The explanation is that He is building quite a different house from the one you thought of – throwing out a new wing here, putting on an extra floor there, running up towers, making courtyards. You thought you were going to be made into a decent little cottage: but He is building a palace. He intends to come and live in it Himself.[1]

This is exactly the point that understanding sonship helps us to grasp with great clarity. We should not be surprised that the way to our destiny is marked by God's wise providence and his daring purposes of restoring *in us* the image of his Son, and therefore *his own glory*. Jesus prayed for this: 'Father, I want those you have given me to be with me where I am, and to see my glory, the glory you have given me because you loved me before the creation of the world' (*Jn. 17:24*).

3. *Conformity*. Paul says that God's sons will be conformed to the likeness of Christ. *Conformity* is another significant word in the New Testament. It belongs to a family of words that mean to shape or mould something. Paul says that we will be remoulded to be like Christ. The use of this family of words gives us a clue to the manner in which this takes place.

We are moulded by the Spirit. 'We, who with unveiled faces all reflect [or contemplate] the Lord's glory, are being *transformed* into his likeness with ever-increasing glory, *which comes from the Lord, who is the Spirit*'

[1] C. S. Lewis, *Mere Christianity* (London: William Collins, 1970), p. 172.

(*2 Cor. 3:18*). His specific role is to reshape our lives until we finally express the perfect glory of the Lord.

How does the Spirit accomplish this? Again, it is Paul who has best expressed it. His desire, he said to the Philippians, was to be conformed to Christ's death (*Phil. 3:10*). This is what the Spirit does: he shapes our lives as though the cross of Christ were the mould into which they were being poured in order that, when it has done its work in us, we might reflect his image. The Spirit brings the power of Christ's death for sin to bear on our lives, so that cleansed from sin we will live in obedience to God; he brings the power of Christ's victory over sin's reign to us so that we may share in his victory. He leads us, as he led Jesus, into times of testing, so that we may be purified and live lives of holiness. Peter spoke from personal experience when he said: 'Since Christ suffered in his body, arm yourselves also with the same attitude, because he who has suffered in his body is done with sin. As a result, he does not live the rest of his earthly life for evil human desires, but rather for the will of God' (*1 Pet. 4:1–2*). This is always to be the lifestyle of the children of God who have been brought under the transforming influences of the Holy Spirit.

There is another element in our being conformed to Christ. We ourselves have a responsibility to participate in the work which the Spirit is doing, and to use the means which the Father has given to us to reach the goal of likeness to Jesus Christ as our Elder Brother.

Paul says we are transformed as we 'reflect' or 'contemplate' the Lord's glory. How do we do this? Primarily by looking at the Lord as he has revealed himself in Scripture. It is only as our lives are in line with Scripture, and as our minds are devoted to understanding and applying it obediently, that this reflection of Christ takes place. This produces the renewing of the mind which Paul describes elsewhere (*Rom. 12:1–2*).

Notice that such renewal is the opposite of being conformed to the image the world desires to produce in our lives. Conformity to Christ, through the use of the renewed mind, always produces nonconformists! But Christians are not nonconformists in order to be difficult, or even simply for the sake of being different. Rather, we are nonconformists because we conform to the image of our Lord Jesus Christ. This new attitude of mind emerges from the fact that we are new men and women, children of God 'created to be like God in true righteousness and holiness' (*Eph. 4:23–24*).

4. *Incompleteness.* The process of transformation is, so far, incomplete. We are not yet fully changed into the likeness of Christ. There lies the tension in spiritual experience. We are not what we used to be, thanks to the grace of God, but, on the other hand, we are not yet what God has destined us to be. These twin facts have great significance for us.

This is why the present stage of God's working is marked by 'groaning'!

Creation is groaning (Rom. 8:22), because only when the sons of God are finally manifested as image-bearers of God will it be set free from its bondage to decay. It is 'in the pains of childbirth'. Out of the final regeneration of all things will emerge the finishing touches of God's transforming work in the lives of his sons (*Phil. 1:6*). The cosmic renewal and the final transformation of God's children go hand in hand.

God's children groan as well! (See *Rom. 8:23*.) We are waiting eagerly 'for the adoption of sons', when, in the resurrection, our whole being will share in the new life of the risen Christ, who is our Elder Brother. Then we will bear the full family likeness of the sons of God (*1 Cor. 15:49, Phil. 3:21*). This is not a groan of despair; it is a groan of hope. And because we already have the firstfruits of the Spirit, the adoption certificate and guarantee, we know that our hope will not be disappointed (*Rom. 5:5*).

The Spirit also groans! (See *Rom. 8:26*.) He helps us in our weakness, and sustains us in our moments of need. Although our greatest and most obvious privilege as children is prayer, there are times when we do not know how to pray. Then the Spirit intercedes for us with groanings that cannot be uttered (*8:26–27*).

So, there is indeed tension as we look forward to the final curtain on our lives and on human history. Sometimes that tension reaches such a pitch that we feel it is almost unbearable. We ask: 'Why is it that God's Spirit does not release us from the tension?'

Sometimes we are told that if we only were filled with the Spirit, all tensions would vanish. However, the very fact that the Spirit lives in our lives as the Spirit of sonship is what causes the tension! Without his presence we would not have the firstfruits of the Spirit; we would not be the children of God. We would be so totally a part of this world that the family of God and the world to come would mean nothing whatsoever to us. And we would be strangers to grace. We would not experience the conflict between the kingdom of God and the kingdoms of the world. Again and again we need to remind ourselves that we experience many tensions in our spiritual pilgrimage, not in spite of the fact that we are sons and have the Spirit of adoption, but precisely because we are sons!

5. *Certainty*. God encourages us in the long, slow process of transformation to full sonship. He has predestined us to be conformed to the image of his Son! Christ has prayed that we may share in his glory! Not only so, but the ultimate reason for our salvation and spiritual transformation further guarantees that we will successfully pass through the dangers and trials of the Christian life.

For God's purpose is that Christ should be the firstborn in an innumerable company of brothers!

There is rich blessing and encouragement for us in our salvation, but it is all for God's glory and for the pleasure of his Son, Jesus Christ. Since in Christ we are more than conquerors (*Rom. 8:37*), we can receive the promise Christ himself has given: 'To him who overcomes, I will give the right to sit with me on my throne, just as I overcame and sat down with my Father on his throne' (*Rev. 3:21*). Then the blessings of the covenant that God makes with all his sons will be fulfilled: 'He who overcomes will inherit all this, and I will be his God and he will be my son' (*21:7*).

At last, Father and son will be fully and finally united in eternal fellowship! We will share in the regeneration of all things toward which the whole creation moves under the sovereign direction of God the Father. In the meantime, as God's children, we are being

> *Changed from glory into glory,*
> *Till in heaven we take our place,*
> *Till we cast our crowns before thee,*
> *Lost in wonder, love and praise.*
>
> Charles Wesley

Then, we who now enjoy the liberty of the grace of God, will enjoy forever the liberty of the glory of the children of God (*Rom. 8:21*). For 'now we are children of God, and what we will be has not yet been made known. But we know that when he appears, we shall be like him, for we shall see him as he is' (*1 Jn. 3:2*).

Do *you* think of your relationship to God in terms of a son with his loving, forgiving Father? Or do you still think of yourself as the Father's 'hired servant' (*Lk. 15:19*)?